Introduction

Congratulations! You've successf~~ully~~
dating scene, found your ~~partner~~
to get married. By ~~now~~
you're no idiot, be~~cause~~
what the most impo~~rtant~~
day is—your weddin~~g~~

You probably know ho~~w easy it~~ is for couples to get
caught up in the chaos of choosing hors d'oeuvres
and cake flavors, centerpieces and DJs. The wedding vows are often shoved to the bottom of the
checklist. After all, vows—the words you'll use to
bind your lives together—don't need a deposit to
be paid or a contract signed.

"We'll do it later," couples reason. "We'll both
write something spectacular that perfectly suits our
union … after we decide whether the bridesmaids
should all wear the same style shoe." I have seen
couples furiously scribbling notes and rehearsing
wedding vows right up until the wedding bells are
chiming.

This book is here to help make selecting or writing
your perfect wedding vows both easy and fun.
From traditional vows to religious vows to original
vows, I help you create the best way for you to say
"I do."

Throughout these pages, I give you plenty of
sample vows, quotes, and Bible and other religious
text passages to use for inspiration. And I ask lots
of questions about your partner, your relationship,

and your goals. Answering these questions will help bring out the writer—and the romantic—in you to help you craft the perfect wedding vows for your unique union.

Nuptial Notes

Throughout the text I added sidebars of extra information. Be sure to check these out.

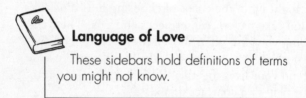

Language of Love

These sidebars hold definitions of terms you might not know.

Nuptial Nuggets

Check out these boxes for interesting facts and fun extra information.

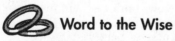

Word to the Wise

Don't skip these sidebars, as they contain tips, advice, and even some cautions you should be aware of.

A Note on Bible Passages

Unless otherwise noted, all Bible verses were excerpted from the NIV Study Bible.

Acknowledgments

I'd like to thank my husband, Christopher, for giving me the encouragement and confidence to take on this challenge, and for putting up with many lonely nights and weekends while I worked on it. Thanks also to my married friends and family who graciously allowed me to share their wedding stories and vows with the world, most especially Kielynn-Marie and Luis Andrés, Lisa and Hank Brown, Jean and Ed Cottrell, Kim and Chris Guarino, Laura and Curt Jacobi, Michelle and Tim Kennedy, Betsy and Gregg Lanyard, Faye and Jerry Macieszek, Amy and Mike Przywara, Amy and B. J. Shell, Lyn and Ryan Stadler, Nancy and Rungsee Suvansri, and Carol Weir and Carlos Chacón.

Also, thanks to my agent, Kim Lionetti, senior acquisitions editor Randy Ladenheim-Gil, development editor Christy Wagner, and copy editor Emily Bell.

And finally to my parents, for believing in me wholeheartedly and unconditionally.

Trademarks

The Wedding Vow: Why "We Do" What "We Do"

In This Chapter

- Thinking about your marriage
- Learning from couples past
- Understanding the wedding vow

Planning a wedding often can seem like an endless checklist of contracts to sign and colors to choose. How do you decide on a cake flavor both of you love? How much is the deposit for the caterer? And where's that list you made of songs the DJ is absolutely forbidden to play at the reception?

They don't call it the "big day" for nothing! Even in the simplest, most casual ceremonies, the bride and groom still have a million decisions to make. In the chaos and confusion of ironing out so many details, couples can sometimes overlook the most important detail of all. Because when it comes right down to it, the wedding is really about one thing: the wedding vows.

The exchanging of vows is what all this wedding fuss is about. Without the wedding vows, there's no reason for a beautiful gown or an expensive band or matching bridesmaids dresses.

It's important for couples to set aside some time during the wedding planning to learn about what the wedding vows symbolize. In this chapter, I let you in on the history and significance of wedding vows—and why they should be such a prominent part of planning your big day.

What's a Wedding Vow?

To understand what the wedding vow is, it's essential to understand the significance of the word *vow*. A vow is a solemn promise or pledge made to another person or to God.

Words such as *solemn* and *pledge* and *dedication* can give you an idea of the seriousness of a vow. When you vow to do something, you're not saying, "I'll give it a shot." You're saying, "I commit myself fully to do this." A vow is a serious, beautiful, personal challenge.

My friend Laura says she was very aware of just how solemn the wedding vows are—and that intensity is written all over her face on her wedding video.

"When you watch our wedding video when I'm saying the vows, I take a long pause and blink really hard between each one," Laura says. "I was serious about those vows and was saying them with everything I had. My family jokes now because I appear so intense."

Language of Love _____

   Solemn is defined as "sacred in character, serious, or grave; deeply earnest."
Webster's New World Dictionary makes
the word's weightiness clear by describing
it as "very impressive or arousing feelings
of awe because of its great importance
and seriousness."

A Promise Is a Promise

When you make a vow to someone, you promise
something to that person unconditionally. To better
understand this, think about how you use the word
promise in your everyday life. You promise a friend
you'll keep a secret. You promise a parent you'll call
home when you arrive at your destination. These
promises are not said under any conditions. You
don't promise to keep the secret unless another
friend asks what the secret is and really seems to
want to know. You don't promise to call home
unless you're too tired or it's too inconvenient to
pick up the phone and tell your mother you're alive
and well.

The people you make these promises to expect
that you will hold up your end of the bargain. After
all, "a promise is a promise." Keeping a promise
strengthens the bonds between two people. Conversely, a promise that's made but not kept is an
empty one and leads to distrust and disappointment.

Promises made on your wedding day are similar in that they are meant to be unconditional and unending. You're essentially saying to your spouse that no matter what happens down the line, you will honor and love and trust him or her.

You don't use words such as *if* and *unless* when speaking about life with your future spouse, because the idea of a marriage vow does not need such caveats. (Of course, this only works if both people keep their promises.)

The Weight of Words

Every wedding is unique, because every couple is unique. Attend 100 different weddings, and you'll see 100 different combinations of food, fun, and love. But you'll find a few common elements at just about every one of those nuptials, and the wedding vows are first on that list.

Nuptial Nuggets _____

Exchanging wedding vows is not part of every culture's customs. In many Native American tribes, the marriage was sealed with a simple exchange of gifts. In some Northern California tribes, if the groom couldn't pay what the bride's parents considered full price for their daughter, he would pay half and live under his in-laws' roof, obeying their rules. This was called a "half-marriage."

But why all the fuss about wedding vows? Aren't they just a few words in the middle of the ceremony where the bride and groom promise "to have and to hold ... till death do us part"?

Yes ... and no.

They are just words, it's true. Your actions down the line as a married couple will speak far louder than those words ever could. But your wedding vows are among the most significant words you will ever utter. You want them to be the right ones for you and your relationship!

These days, many couples are incorporating a lot of their personalities into their wedding ceremonies. Favorite songs are sung, poems are read, and sometimes wedding guests are asked to get in on the act. A recent trend is for each wedding guest to release butterflies or blow bubbles into the air at the end of the ceremony.

As much fun as your wedding should be, the solemnity of that day should not go unnoticed. It is, after all, the first day of a new life you have chosen to live, with a partner to whom you are promising a great deal.

However, none of this should intimidate a newly engaged couple. You may not realize it, but you've probably unknowingly been composing your wedding vows—an essential blueprint for your marriage—in your head and in your heart for some time.

Word to the Wise

To get your wedding guests into the spirit of the day, pick a spot during your ceremony to ask all married couples to rise and hold hands while the officiant delivers a marriage blessing or recommitment prayer. This is a unique way for every married couple to walk away from your nuptials feeling like their own marriage has been made a special focus of the day.

After all, in choosing a life partner, you have declared in your heart that this is the person you want in your life forever. This is the one you want to wake up next to every morning, the one who will shoulder your sorrows and rejoice in your successes. And this is the one for whom you will do the same.

When couples get engaged, they are saying to each other, "I will": "I will be there for you through thick and thin." "I will respect you and love you and honor you, and only you."

On your wedding day, those "I will" promises change to the more formal, more emphatic "I do." But the intentions, born way before you walk down the aisle, are the same.

To Have and To Hold: History of Marriage

In ancient times, marriages were created based more on economic reasons and proximity than love and romance. Often they were arranged by family members, with a *dowry* paid by the bride or a *bride-price* paid by the groom.

Language of Love

A **dowry** is the property (land, cash, or goods) a woman brings to her husband for marriage. The tradition was outlawed in India in 1961 but continues there and elsewhere today, sometimes resulting in the death of the bride if the dowry is considered insufficient by the groom. A **bride-price** is the money and property given to a prospective bride's family by the groom and his family.

In many cultures, the groom actually captured the bride; he literally took her from her parents' home and brought her to his. This probably isn't what a woman had in mind when she said she wanted someone to "sweep her off her feet"!

To this day, for various reasons, some cultures still incorporate a symbolic "bridal capture" element into their more contemporary wedding rituals.

Nuptial Nuggets

When bridal capture was a popular way to "settle down," the groom would bring along several of his strongest friends to help fend off the bride's family members who tried to keep her from being taken. These buff boys were the world's first groomsmen. These days, a groomsman's biggest job is planning the bachelor party. This task often entails making the groom happy while at the same time trying to avert potential disaster. Perhaps there's a certain symmetry to groomsmen past and present.

In the Ukraine, for example, a bride may be briefly "kidnapped" by her friends during the wedding reception. For Ukrainians, this lighthearted tradition symbolizes the invasions their country has endured over the years.

Working for Your Woman

Sometimes a groom agreed to work for the bride's family for a certain length of time to earn the right to his bride. The biblical story of Jacob (Genesis 29:14–30) illustrates the practice of earning one's wife through working for her father:

> Jacob was in love with Rachel and said, "I'll work for you for seven years in return for your

younger daughter Rachel." … So Jacob served seven years to get Rachel, but they seemed like only a few days to him because of his love for her. (Genesis 29:18, 20)

In the days of Jacob and Rachel, the sharing of the marriage bed, or "marriage chamber," formed the bond between husband and wife. There were no elaborate vows to speak, but feasting and singing often were used to express the families' new bonds and to offer blessings for the new couple.

 Nuptial Nuggets

In many cultures, the marriage bed is still important to the pomp and circumstance of the wedding day. In Iceland, for instance, the bridesmaids undress the bride and place her on the wedding bed wearing nothing but the traditional wedding headdress. The groom then enters and removes the headdress, and the priest blesses the couple one last time. Talk about three's a crowd!

Although the marriage bed doesn't hold quite the significance today that it used to, those celebratory feasts between families or whole tribes are still around. They've turned into the modern-day wedding reception, complete with dinner, DJs, and the occasional line dance.

The Times They Are A-Changin'

Long ago, much attention was paid to the couple's possessions, or whose land they received to live on. Not much was spelled out about what the husband would do to care for his wife, or what the wife would do to show her love for her husband.

It was implied that the wife was the husband's property and that she was to serve him dutifully and faithfully and bear him children. In return, the husband was to provide adequate shelter, food, and safety for his wife and their family.

Over the course of many generations, women became less like property and more like equals in the eyes of their beloveds. Society changed, and with it, so did marriage. Weddings became more about love and less about land and livestock.

And with those changes came a more formal exchanging of vows. Today, the wedding day is a symbolic joining of two hearts as much as it is a joining of two lives, two families, and two futures.

The Ways We Wed

The idea of two becoming one through the vows of marriage has been expressed in different ways throughout the world. In many cultures, brides and grooms were—and still are—literally bound together in some way for the ceremony, a practice known as *handfasting*.

Language of Love

Handfasting is a betrothal signaled by the joining of hands. Different cultures express this tradition in different ways. In Celtic tradition, the couple's wrists are tied together in a "love knot," which is where the expression "tying the knot" comes from!

Sometimes handfasting is used in a secular ceremony as a way to symbolize the joining of two people. In these handfasting ceremonies, the couple publicly agrees to be joined together for a year and a day, at which time they can opt to "renew" their handfasting commitment or get married legally.

In the Hindu culture, the bride's and groom's hands are sometimes tied together with a string in a ritual called Hasthagranthi. In Mexico, a rosary or white rope is wound around the couple's shoulders in a figure eight, symbolizing their union for eternity. And in Egypt, the wedding rings are tied together during the ceremony using a rope that was first looped around the groom's body.

Christian pastors have used Ecclesiastes 4:12 to illustrate that the Bible takes the symbolic knot-tying one step further: "Though one may be overpowered, two can defend themselves. A cord of three strands is not quickly broken."

Marriage, Christians say, is strongest when it is created using a cord of three strands—husband, wife, and God.

Fast Forward: Why We Still Take Vows

Gone are the days of the groom paying a dowry for his bride. (Although some may argue that the amount spent on a woman's engagement ring, and subsequent wedding of her dreams, feels like a dowry to his bank account!) And you'd be hard-pressed to find a groom willing to work for his future father-in-law for months or even years before he could wed the woman of his dreams. (Not that women aren't worth it, mind you.)

Today, love and romance factor highest into most marriage equations. Men and women want to spend the rest of their lives with someone who stimulates them mentally, emotionally, and physically.

In some respects, husbands and wives demand much more of each other now than in centuries past. This should mean they also give much more of themselves in terms of sacrifice and commitment. The wedding vows are meant to spell out just what they're willing to give.

Wedding vows go beyond the fact that you have similar hobbies and aspirations. The vows speak to the very heart of your union, the magic that has made you two separate people stronger as a unit.

They also spell out how you plan to keep that unit intact.

The traditional Christian rites of marriage list the wedding vows as "the Declaration of Intention." Essentially, the wedding vows define the couple's marriage: who it is for, what it will be, and what it will include.

Imagine buying a car and expecting it to run even though you have not committed to keeping gas in the tank. Chances are, you're not going to get very far, no matter how much you love the car. Such is married life without having exchanged wedding vows. Because like that shiny new car, you need plenty of fuel to make a marriage last.

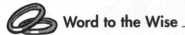 **Word to the Wise**

> Wedding vows are not meant to be laundry lists of everyday things you and your spouse are willing to do for each other. Instead of including such things in your wedding vows, make separate lists of such expectations, and share these with your partner long before the big day. This will give both bride and groom a glimpse into what the other is imagining everyday married life will be like.

Have you ever seen a bride and groom break down in tears when they begin to exchange wedding vows? There's something about the words "to have and to hold, from this day forward" that can take even the most stoic groom and reduce him to a sappy puddle of love. In those simple words, he is declaring his undying devotion to his beloved. And that is such a beautiful thing!

When Hank and Lisa got married, nobody was surprised when Lisa got emotional while saying her vows to Hank. But the wedding guests were all taken aback when the usually stoic Hank choked up while pledging his love to her—to the point where he could barely recite his lines.

Says Hank: "Something about saying those words, 'to have and to hold, from this day forward' … and looking into the eyes of my future wife, it was just the happiest moment of my life."

It is a ritual nearly as old as time itself, yet surprisingly reborn with each and every new "I do."

The Least You Need to Know

- Wedding vows are solemn promises you make to your spouse.
- Marriage has evolved from being about property and proximity to being more about love and romance.
- The words you use in your wedding vows are the foundation for your marriage.

"I Pledge Allegiance": Wedding Vows of Different Religions

In This Chapter

- Understanding what wedding vows mean to Christians
- Learning Jewish wedding traditions
- Learning about Muslim wedding elements
- Discovering the wedding traditions of Eastern religions
- Crafting vows for the nonreligious

It's said that the language of love is universal. The institution of marriage is, in some ways, proof of this. After all, some basic tenets of marriage cross all religious and ethnic borders. Faithfulness, mutual support, and honesty are a few of the many common principles brides and grooms typically vow to uphold, whether they're standing at the altar or under the chuppah.

But the language of marriage is as varied as the religious beliefs of people in all four corners of the world. There are many different ways to tie the knot, and a lot of them are based on the world's major religions. For some people, marriage is not just the joining of two lives—it is the joining of two souls, brought together by God, in part to fulfill one of God's wishes for his people.

In this chapter, I explain the differences among wedding vows for major religions, as well as how those vows take on a slightly different meaning for secular wedding ceremonies.

Holy Matrimony!: Christianity and the Wedding Vow

The concept of joining a man and a woman into one unit is as old as the Bible's first male and female, Adam and Eve. When God created Eve using Adam's rib, Adam remarks that this new being is truly a part of him. The Old Testament text takes this observation one step further in Genesis 2:24:

> For this reason a man will leave his father and mother and be united to his wife, and they will become one flesh.

Of course, nothing in that passage spells out the rules for this union. But one could say that this passage indicates that marriage is something God wants for us.

Nuptial Nuggets

Some say the marriage of Adam and Eve was the most blessed of all unions. After all, Eve didn't have any mother-in-law standards to try to live up to, and no over-protective father-of-the-bride was standing over Adam with a watchful eye. The Garden of Eden was paradise indeed!

A clearer idea of marriage as a Christian sacrament, as something holy, can be traced to St. Paul in Ephesians 5:22–32. Paul likened the relationship between husband and wife to the covenant between Christ and the church:

> Wives, submit to your husbands as to the Lord. For the husband is the head of the wife as Christ is the head of the church ... Now as the church submits to Christ, so also wives should submit to their husbands in everything.
>
> Husbands love your wives, just as Christ loved the church and gave himself up for her to make her holy ... In this same way husbands ought to love their wives as their own bodies ... (Ephesians 5:22–26 and 28)

The passage is sometimes dismissed by today's couples, particularly brides, as outdated and even sexist. But others interpret the text as implying that both parties should be equally submissive to the other.

Whether you take the passage literally or figuratively, most *Christians* agree that one underlying point Paul makes is that marriage is a holy union. As such, wedding vows are made in the presence of God, who essentially becomes part of that union.

Language of Love

A **Christian** is a person who believes in Christianity, the monotheistic religion that recognizes Jesus as the messiah and follows his teachings.

I attended a wedding once in which the pastor spoke frankly to the bride and groom of how upholding the vows of their marriage was important not only because they were promising each other they would, but because they were promising God they would. It seems like a heavy thing to say, but I have spoken to couples for whom those words have helped them through troubles that otherwise may have crumbled the marriage.

One *Catholic* friend stuck with her marriage during considerable stress because, as she put it, "Even when I felt like maybe I shouldn't or couldn't stay committed to my husband, I stayed committed to the marriage. I stayed committed to God."

Language of Love

Catholic (with a lowercase "c") means "universal" or "whole." The **Catholic faith** includes those in the universal Christian Church headed by the pope, such as the Roman, Greek Orthodox, or Anglo-Catholic denominations.

Most Christian wedding vows reflect this promise to keep one's marriage intact through thick and thin. The vows stress that no matter what happens, each is committed to the other. The following sample vows illustrate this overall theme of mutual commitment. The most well-known and most commonly used wedding vow is found in the Episcopal Church's 1662 Book of Common Prayer:

> I _____, take thee _____ to be my wedded Husband, to have and to hold from this day forward, for better for worse, for richer for poorer, in sickness and in health, to love and to cherish, till death us do part, according to God's holy ordinance; and thereto I give thee my troth.

Modifications of this vow are used in several Christian denominations.

Suggested vows for the Presbyterian Church:

I, _____, take thee _____, to be my wedded wife/husband, and I do promise and covenant, before God and these witnesses, to be thy loving and faithful wife/husband; in plenty and in want, in joy and in sorrow, in sickness and in health, as long as we both shall live.

Suggested vows for the Roman Catholic:

I, _____, take you, _____, to be my husband. I promise to be true to you in good times and bad, in sickness and in health. I will love you and honor you all the days of my life.

Suggested vows for the United Church:

_____, I take you to be my wife, to laugh with you in joy, to grieve with you in sorrow, to grow with you in love, serving mankind in peace and hope, as long as we both shall live.

In reading the vows listed here, you might be struck by the absence of the standard wedding words "I do." When people think of traditional wedding vows, "I do" often come to mind. Actually, the part of the ceremony where bride and groom agree to the marriage with those famous words is called the "Declaration of Intention," and happens before the wedding vows are exchanged. (See Chapter 3 for the elements of a traditional wedding ceremony.)

During the "Declaration of Intention," the officiant asks the bride and groom whether each agrees to be married to each other, and the standard response is "I do." Then the officiant typically moves on to the actual exchanging of vows, rings, and any other symbolic elements the couple wishes to include.

Often the "Declaration of Intention" leads directly into the exchanging of vows and rings, so all three elements combine to form the main part of the marriage rite.

These wedding vows from the Baptist Church (said by both groom and bride) illustrate this traditional flow of the Christian wedding ceremony elements:

> *Pastor:* Will you, _____, have _____ to be your wife? Will you love her, comfort and keep her, and forsaking all other remain true to her as long as you both shall live?
>
> *Groom:* I will.
>
> I, _____, take thee _____, to be my wife, and before God and these witnesses I promise to be a faithful and true husband.
>
> *(Rings)* With this ring I thee wed, and all my worldly goods I thee endow. In sickness and in health, in poverty or in wealth, till death do us part.

And this one, from the Catholic Church, as spoken by both groom and bride:

Priest: _____, will you take _____ here present, for your lawful husband according to the rite of our Holy Mother, the Catholic Church?

Bride: I will.

I, _____, take you _____, for my husband, to have and to hold, from this day forward, for better, for worse, for richer, for poorer, in sickness and in health, until death do us part.

(Rings) With this ring I thee wed, and pledge thee my troth.

The Ketubah: The Jewish Marriage Contract

To *Jews*, marriage is a special gift God wants for his people. It is the basis for Jewish community, for the continuation of the Jewish race, and for the continued oneness with God.

Language of Love

A **Jew** is a member of a cultural community whose religion is Judaism, the monotheistic religion based on the teachings of the Old Testament, the Torah, and the Talmud.

Marriage is the fulfillment of a Jewish command-ment, "*p'ru u'rvu*," be fruitful and multiply. Rab-binic tradition teaches that a marriage will only be peaceful if God is a part of the union.

There is no "I do" moment in Jewish weddings as there is in Christian ceremonies. But Jewish wed-dings are full of tradition and symbolism and can include the exchanging of personal wedding vows, if the couple so desires.

Nuptial Nuggets

To understand how important and holy marriage is in Judaism, consider this: the Hebrew word for man is *EISH*, spelled Aleph-Yud-Shin. The Hebrew word for woman is *EISHA*, spelled Aleph-Shin-Hay. The letters *Yud* and *Hay* combine to form the Hebrew name for God. Removing the letters *Yud* and *Hay* (God) from the words *EISH* and *EISHA* leaves the letters *Aleph* and *Shin*. *Aleph* and *Shin* spell ESH, which is the word for fire.

Jewish wedding traditions vary depending on the group of Judaism to which the bride and/or groom belong. Orthodox, Conservative, and Reform Jews all have different beliefs and traditions when it comes to the marriage rite. Orthodox and most Conservative Jews conduct the ceremony in

Hebrew, so keep in mind that your guests might appreciate a translation of the main elements (in a program given to them at the synagogue) if many of them do not speak that language.

With slight variations, all Jewish weddings are made of two parts: the first, called *kiddushin* or *erusin*, is the betrothal ceremony; the second, *nissuin*, is the marriage ceremony.

Kiddushin formalizes the taking of the bride by the groom, and the acceptance of the groom by his chosen wife. A traditional kiddushin ceremony includes a gift of a ring from the groom to his bride.

Nuptial Nuggets

In ancient times, kiddushin was more of a legal ceremony, binding the woman to her mate as his property. It was held up to a year before the second ceremony, which celebrated the joining of the two people and the holiness of the union. Eventually, kiddushin became more of a symbolic "taking" of the bride and was combined with the marriage ceremony.

When the ring is given, the groom often recites a Hebrew vow declaring his bride's commitment to him:

> Behold, thou art consecrated to me with this ring, according to the law of Moses and Israel.

Nuptial Nuggets

The role of women in marriage has long been a reflection of how women were viewed in society in general. This crosses most religious lines. In an Orthodox Jewish wedding ceremony, for example, the woman says nothing, merely accepting her husband's decree to take her as his property. Many of today's Jewish couples look for ways to make their wedding ceremonies more egalitarian without losing the sentiment of a ceremony steeped in tradition.

The second part of the ceremony, nissuin, centers on seven blessings for the bride and groom, celebrating their union and thanking God for creating it.

It is between these two ceremonies—after the ring exchange and before the blessings—that a more contemporary exchange of wedding vows may take place in the form of reading the *ketubah*, the Jewish marriage contract.

Language of Love

Ketubah (plural: *ketubot*) literally means "writing" or "written." This Jewish marriage contract was traditionally written in Aramaic, the language of the Talmud, and signed by two male witnesses. Jewish couples are forbidden to live together without a ketubah.

Under Jewish law, the ketubah is what binds a couple together in holy matrimony. Historically, it was a document that outlined the husband's obligations to his wife. It was signed by the groom and then kept by the bride as a form of insurance in case of death or divorce. In that regard, the ancient document has been called the world's first prenuptial agreement!

The ketubah is traditionally written in Hebrew, though some couples opt to have theirs translated into English as well. It has become tradition to decorate the ketubah and hang it in the home as precious artwork and a constant reminder of a couple's binding commitment to each other.

Over time, couples have taken more initiative when choosing the type of artwork and the words to include in their ketubot. Some choose to keep the traditional language of the ancient ketubah, written thousands of years ago, but plenty of modern couples elect to blend those time-tested words with their own more contemporary thoughts.

Still others choose to have two ketubot: a traditional public one to include as part of the ceremony, and a separate private one that comprises their personal vows to each other.

Here's an example of the traditional Orthodox Ketubah text:

> On the _____ day of the week, the day of the [Hebrew] month of _____, the year _____ after the creation of the world, according to the manner in which we count [dates] here in the community of _____, the bridegroom _____ son of _____ said to this virgin _____ daughter of _____, "Be my wife according to the law of Moses and Israel. I will work, honor, feed, and support you in the custom of Jewish men, who work, honor, feed, and support their wives faithfully. I will give you the settlement (*mohar*) of virgins, two hundred silver *zuzim*, which is due you according to Torah law, as well as your food, clothing, necessities of life, and conjugal needs, according to the universal custom."
>
> Miss _____ agreed, and became his wife. This dowry that she brought from her father's house, whether in silver, gold, jewelry, clothing, home furnishings, or bedding, Mr. _____, our bridegroom, accepts as being worth one hundred silver pieces (*zekukim*).
>
> Our bridegroom, Mr. _____ agreed, and of his own accord, added an additional one

hundred silver pieces *(zekukim)* paralleling the above. The entire amount is then two hundred silver pieces *(zekukim)*.

Mr. _____ our bridegroom made this declaration: "The obligation of this marriage contract *(kethubah)*, this dowry, and this additional amount, I accept upon myself and upon my heirs after me. It can be paid from the entire best part of the property and possessions that I own under all the heavens, whether I own [this property] already, or will own it in the future. [It includes] both mortgageable property and nonmortgageable property. All of it shall be mortgaged and bound as security to pay this marriage contract, this dowry, and this additional amount. [It can be taken] from me, even from the shirt on my back, during my lifetime, and after my lifetime, from this day and forever."

The obligation of this marriage contract, this dowry, and this additional amount was accepted by Mr. _____, our bridegroom, according to all the strictest usage of all marriage contracts and additional amounts that are customary for daughters of Israel, according to the ordinances of our sages, of blessed memory. [It shall] not be a mere speculation or a sample document.

We have made a *kinyan* from Mr. _____ son of _____ our bridegroom, to Miss _____ daughter of _____, this virgin, regarding everything written and stated above, with an article that is fit for such a *kinyan*.

And everything is valid and confirmed.

The following sample ketubah has a slightly more contemporary feel:

> We witness that on the _____ day of the week, the _____ day of the month of _____, in the year _____, corresponding to the _____ day of _____, here in _____:

> The bride, _____, daughter of _____, says to the groom: "With this ring you are consecrated unto me as my husband, according to the tradition of Moses and the Jewish people. I shall treasure you, nourish you, support you, and respect you as Jewish women have devoted themselves to their husbands, with integrity."

> The groom, _____, son of _____, says to the bride: "With this ring you are consecrated unto me as my wife, according to the tradition of Moses and the Jewish people. I shall treasure you, nourish you, support you, and respect you as Jewish men have devoted themselves to their wives, with integrity."

> "We promise to try to be ever open to one another while cherishing each other's uniqueness; to comfort and challenge each other

through life's sorrow and joy; to share our intuition and insight with one another; and above all, to do everything within our power to permit each of us to become the persons we are yet to be.

"We also pledge to establish a home open to the spiritual potential in all life; a home wherein the flow of the seasons and the passages of life are celebrated through the symbols of Jewish heritage; a home filled with reverence for learning, loving, and generosity; a home wherein ancient melody, candles, and wine sanctify the table; a home joined ever more closely to the community of Israel. This marriage has been authorized also by the civil authorities of _____. It is valid and binding."

Not all Jewish couples choose to read their ketubah at the wedding. Again, much depends on the sect of Judaism to which the bride and groom belong.

Muslim Wedding Vows

According to *Islam*, marriage is considered "half of one's faith." Allah taught that the very foundation of society is marriage. There is no celibacy in Islam, unlike the revered priests and nuns in Catholicism. On the contrary, marriage is viewed as a safeguard against moral lapses. In this way, it is seen as a religious commandment as well as a social necessity.

Language of Love

Islam is the monotheistic religion of Muslims. The supreme deity is Allah and the chief prophet and founder is Muhammad. The basics of the religion are detailed in the holy book the Koran.

The Koran expresses the importance of marriage in several ways:

> And among His signs is this, that He created for you mates from among yourselves, that you may dwell in tranquility with them, and He has put love and mercy between your hearts. Undoubtedly in these are signs for those who reflect. (30:21)

Many Muslim marriages are arranged, with a ceremony held in the bride's home or in a mosque. They are family celebrations that often last 4 to 7 days and include many rituals and ceremonies.

The traditional Muslim ceremony entails the officiant explaining to the bride and groom what their commitment to each other means, to which they acknowledge their consent. There is not usually a formal exchanging of vows.

However, the ceremony traditionally includes this exchange:

Bride: I, _____, offer you myself in marriage in accordance with the instructions of the Holy Koran and the Holy Prophet, peace and blessing be upon Him. I pledge, in honesty and with sincerity, to be for you an obedient and faithful wife.

Groom: I pledge, in honesty and with sincerity, to be for you a faithful and helpful husband.

Eastern Religion Wedding Vows

Wedding ceremonies for Eastern religions such as Buddhism and Hinduism are filled with symbolism and tradition. Everyone—wedding party, family, as well as guests—gets into the spirit of the event, which can last for several days. Special ceremonies are held for the bride, the groom, and their respective families.

Hindu Wedding Vows

Hindu weddings are colorful events, with many pre-wedding rituals for the bride and groom. The main wedding ceremony can last up to 2 or 3 hours and include the exchanging of garlands, rings, and food.

For Hindus, the wedding vows are exchanged through the ritual of saptapadi, the Seven Steps. For this the couple joins hands and takes seven steps around the marriage fire. With each step, either the bride and groom or the officiant offers seven specific blessings for the marriage, including strength, prosperity, and children. The wording varies with different traditions, but the blessings are the same.

> ### Language of Love
>
> **Hindu** can mean a person born or living in India or on the Indian subcontinent, or a follower of Hinduism, which is an ancient religious tradition of India. Hinduism follows the doctrines of karma (the cumulative effects of a person's actions), dharma (universal law), and samsara (the cycle of rebirth).

Here is one example of the Saptapadi blessings:

Let us take this first step vowing to keep a pure household, avoiding things that might harm us.

Let us take this second step vowing to develop mental, physical and spiritual powers.

Let us take this third step with the aim of increasing our wealth by righteous means.

Let us take this fourth step to acquire knowledge, happiness, and harmony by mutual love and trust.

Let us take this fifth step to pray for virtuous, intelligent, and courageous children.

Let us take this sixth step for longevity.

Let us take this seventh step to vow that we will always remain true companions and life-long partners.

Buddhist Wedding Traditions

In *Buddhism*, weddings are secular events, not tied to a religious significance or doctrine of the faith. As such, there is not one traditional Buddhist wedding ceremony, although Buddhist rituals such as lighting incense and making offerings to Buddha have been used in conjunction with the exchanging of marriage vows.

Language of Love

Buddhism is an Eastern religion and philosophy that teaches that right thinking and self-denial will enable the soul to reach Nirvana, a divine state of release from misdirected desire.

Because Buddhist weddings are social and not religious affairs, there is no assigned set of marriage vows. However, the bride and groom typically recite vows based on the Sigalovada Sutta (the Buddhist guide for the domestic and social life of a layman), which says:

In five ways should a wife, as Western quarter, be ministered to by her husband: by respect, by courtesy, by faithfulness, by handing over authority to her, by providing her with ornaments. In these five ways does the wife minister to by her husband as the Western quarter, love him: her duties are well performed by hospitality to kin of both, by faithfulness, by watching over the goods he brings, and by skill and industry in discharging all business.

Here is a sample of Buddhist wedding vows based on the Sigalovada Sutta:

Groom: For my wife I will love and respect her, be kind and considerate, be faithful, delegate domestic management, and give her gifts to please her.

Bride: For my husband I will be hospitable to my in-laws and friends of my husband, keep a clean and happy home, be faithful, and protect our investments and lovingly discharging my responsibilities.

Secular Wedding Vows

A couple doesn't have to be religious to exchange meaningful vows on their wedding day. After all, the promises you're making come from the heart and are intended to be kept with your beloved in mind.

Secular wedding vows are beautiful in that they focus first and foremost on the faith the couple has in each other. Many secular wedding vows borrow from the traditional religious vows in their wording and overall themes.

Language of Love

Secular is used to describe activities or attitudes that have no religious or spiritual attachment. Secular weddings often are performed by a judge or notary public instead of a clergy member, and the vows contain no religious references.

I have attended secular wedding ceremonies where the bride and groom exchange traditional "To have and to hold, from this day forward, for better or for worse ..." vows, swiped right from the Episcopal Church's Book of Common Prayer. Whether spoken with God in mind or not, there's something to be said for the simplicity and succinctness of those time-tested promises.

But if you're not interested in tradition, the sky's the limit! Couples who opt for a secular wedding have the freedom to do what they please in the ceremony, from start to finish. They need not uphold any rules of any church.

Here are some sample secular wedding vows:

I, _____, take you _____, to be my husband/wife. I promise to be true to you and only you, to love and trust and honor you. I will share your joys and shoulder your sorrows, be a calming presence in your life for both the good times and the bad. I will do my best to bring laughter to your world. I will end each day with you in my dreams and a smile on my face.

I, _____, take you _____, to be my husband/wife, the one I will love and cherish for the rest of my days. For better or for worse, for richer or for poorer, in sickness and in health, you have my unending devotion.

On this day, in the presence of our loved ones, I place my future in your hands with a smile on my face and love in my heart. My commitment to you is unbending and unending; it will fill all the days of my life. I am proud of all that you are and all we will be together. To you, my partner for life, I pledge my friendship, my passion, and my love.

Today I will marry my best friend, the one I laugh with, live for, and love. Your goals are now my goals, your hopes and dreams are my hopes and dreams, and I will do everything in my power to make those dreams come true. I stand here with absolute certainty that in the greatest joys and the deepest sorrows that life has in store for us, we will always find and celebrate the same bonds of love that brought us here today. My life is complete, now and forever, because of you.

We pledge to each other to be loving friends and committed partners: to talk and to listen, to trust and appreciate one another; to respect and cherish each other's uniqueness; and to support, comfort, and strengthen each other through the good times and the bad. We promise to share hopes, thoughts, and dreams as we build our lives together.

The Least You Need to Know

- Christian wedding vows are designed to bind a couple together forever with God as a focal point of the union.
- The Jewish marriage contract is a legal, religious, and romantic document that joins a husband and wife.
- Muslims believe marriage is half of one's faith, though there are no elaborate vows exchanged during the wedding ceremony.
- Wedding vows for Hindu couples involve taking seven steps while asking for blessings of family, fortune, and health.
- Buddhist weddings are social rather than religious affairs.
- Secular wedding vows focus on the loving commitment the two people make to each other.

Chapter 3

Can "I Do" This?: Talking With the Official

In This Chapter

- Selecting the right wedding officiant
- Communicating with your officiant
- Knowing your limits for customizing your vows
- Putting together a wedding ceremony outline

Before you begin crafting the perfect wedding vows or decide which traditional—or not-so-traditional—language you'd like to use on your wedding day, it's important to take a step back from the planning process and think about the big picture. Although you are the "producer" of your wedding, your vision needs to match that of the "director"—the wedding officiant.

The wedding vows may be the most important elements in your wedding ceremony, but they are just one scene in a larger script that includes other vowlike features.

In this chapter, I discuss the importance of speaking with the wedding officiant early on in the planning process, as well as a few of the religious limitations some couples may be up against when designing their unique nuptials. I also introduce the basic wedding ceremony elements so couples can get an idea of the many different ways they can verbalize their lifelong commitment.

Know Your Limits

Christina and David planned their wedding long distance, but they were determined to do everything themselves. They chose to marry in Christina's hometown church, which was in a different state from where they lived. They booked the church and the reception hall and then proceeded to go about finalizing a thousand other details for their big day.

Christina and David did not overlook the importance of their wedding vows. On the contrary, they sat down and crafted what they considered the perfect promises of love and commitment to each other.

Then, the weekend before the wedding, they met with the pastor of the church where they were getting married and presented their vows to him to include in the ceremony. To their surprise, he told them their vows didn't jibe with the church's more traditional views of marriage and had to be revamped.

Christina and David were crushed at this last-minute change of plans, but they were able to rewrite their vows to please the officiant and themselves.

 **Word to the Wise**

> When selecting a wedding site, couples often ask just two questions: Is the site available on the date we've chosen? Are there requirements for a wedding to take place here? Don't be afraid to ask about your other wishes and requirements, right down to the last detail. Better to find out before you order 200 tiny bottles of bubbles for your wedding guests that blowing bubbles after the ceremony is forbidden in the sanctuary.

Their mistake is one many couples make: not communicating well enough—or early enough—with the wedding officiant.

Wedding vows are such personal statements that some couples believe they can say whatever they want. This is true more times than not, but it depends on several factors.

Religious Requirements

Religious weddings are beautiful affairs, in part because the words and elements used hold so much tradition and significance. Knowing that thousands of couples have pledged their lives to each other using the same words and deeds for generations is appealing to many brides and grooms who view that sense of history as a very romantic aspect of their wedding day.

The important thing to remember about the beauty of a religious ceremony is that it has a select framework to it, and every element has been carefully chosen for a specific reason.

Choosing to deviate from that framework is possible in some religious institutions but forbidden in others. Before you get excited and start thinking outside the box when it comes to your wedding vows, it's best to know exactly what is inside the box you have chosen and whether you're allowed to venture out of it at all.

Religion can play a significant part in the wording of the vows and the ceremony itself. Some clergy only allow a couple to use the church's traditional wedding vows. It's essential to discuss how much leeway you have when it comes to writing your own vows or inserting other special elements into the ceremony.

When Amy and BJ got married in a nondenominational church, they didn't mind using the wedding vows traditional to that church—with one exception.

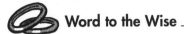 **Word to the Wise** _____

> Many adults know the prayers and liturgies unique to their religion, but they may not know all the meanings behind them. Before you commit to marrying in a particular church, do some research online or in your local library to brush up on your religion's basic beliefs and the beliefs of other religions you think might be similar. Knowing the intricacies of your religion will enable you to ask intelligent questions when meeting with your officiant.

"I refused to say the word *obey*, as part of the 'love, honor, and obey' line in the wedding vows we were given by the pastor," says Amy. "I brought it up with our pastor the first time we met with him, and he was totally on the same page with us on that." Because Amy brought up her concern right away, she and BJ were able to amend the vow to their liking without any hassle.

For Jewish couples, the ceremony details and even the language spoken differs slightly depending on which sect of Judaism—Orthodox, Reform, or Conservative—the couple is marrying in.

The Orthodox Jewish wedding ceremony follows a strict pattern from which it is impossible to deviate. To marry in this tradition, both the bride's and groom's parents must also be Orthodox. And Orthodox rabbis will not marry interfaith couples.

Nuptial Nuggets _____

The first challenge for engaged couples is finding suitable wedding and reception sites that are available in the season the couple wants to marry. For Orthodox Jews, this task is made even tougher by the strict rules for when a wedding can take place. Couples cannot get married in the 49 days between Passover and Pentecost, or during 3 weeks between July and August. It is also forbidden to marry on the Sabbath or on festival days. And if a Saturday wedding is your only option, the ceremony cannot begin earlier than 2 hours after sundown.

Reform and Conservative Jewish brides and grooms have a bit more leeway. For example, in Orthodox wedding ceremonies, the bride is presented with a wedding ring but says nothing. Her acceptance of the ring signifies her commitment to the marriage. In today's Reform and Conservative Jewish ceremonies, however, a bride often is allowed to give her groom a ring, too, and she can recite an appropriate passage of betrothal.

Every denomination has its own rules and traditions. Finding out just what those rules are—and whether they can be bent or broken—is essential to planning the wedding of your dreams.

Church Limitations

For some couples, the first stumbling block comes when selecting a wedding site where both of you are welcome to say "I do." Some Christian churches require that at least one half of the couple be a baptized member of that religious denomination and often a member of that church.

As long as the bride and groom are standing under the *chuppah*, a Jewish wedding ceremony can take place just about anywhere.

Language of Love

The **chuppah** (pronounced *hup-pah*) is a cloth canopy under which a Jewish couple ties the knot. In ancient times, Jewish weddings took place in the groom's tent, and today's symbolic use of the chuppah is meant to signify the couple's new home.

Likewise, most Protestant faiths allow a couple to marry outside of a church if they prefer an outdoor ceremony or something else nontraditional. But the Catholic Church, with rare exception, requires couples to marry in a Catholic sanctuary.

Besides deeming who gets to stand at the altar and say "I do," churches and synagogues set other limitations engaged couples need to be mindful of. Depending on the time of year and how busy the sanctuary is, some churches set time limits for weddings, so be sure to ask about this and plan accordingly when crafting your wedding ceremony and vows.

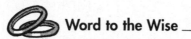

Word to the Wise

One requirement for couples getting married in the Catholic Church is premarital counseling classes, called Pre-Cana. The classes focus on the religious institution of marriage, the importance of sacrifice, and the couple's compatibility and future goals.

Other Christian and Jewish denominations offer similar premarital counseling sessions. Couples who go through these classes should use what they learn when thinking not only about their future but about their wedding vows as well.

I got married in a nondenominational wedding chapel that was rented out by the hour. My husband and I were told upfront that another ceremony was scheduled 2 hours after ours, and we kept that in mind as we planned our nuptials.

Officiants' Demands

Although some wedding ceremonies and vows must follow some hard-and-fast religious rules, the wedding officiant decides much of what can be said and done. Sometimes the trick to getting what you want on your wedding day is to enlist the person who will help you do just that.

Knowing who you are as individuals and as a couple is the first step to finding an officiant who will respect your wishes for the ceremony. And knowing who you are goes hand in hand with setting your priorities.

When couples sit down to plan their wedding day, they often set certain priorities for the reception right off the bat. Some want to serve a top-notch meal; others want to create a fun-loving, party atmosphere.

In a similar way, you should set your priorities for your wedding ceremony so you select the right setting and the right officiant for you. Is the religion or the church most important to you? Is it so important you're willing to give up some freedom of choice when it comes to wording and other elements of your nuptials? Or is that freedom of choice the most important thing to you and your soon-to-be spouse when it comes to the way you will say "I do"?

A friend once told me the story of how she was on the hunt for a new car, one that had all the elements she wanted in the price range she could afford. She was having trouble finding it. Each time she mentioned the search to her mother, her mom would say "Remember, the color doesn't matter. The deal is what is most important."

Nuptial Nuggets

Carol was raised a Christian, but her groom, Carlos, is an atheist. His only request for their wedding ceremony was that it not include any religion at all. To respect this but still have the ceremony that also reflected her beliefs, Carol found a notary public who was eager to please both of them. The officiant suggested an Apache blessing both Carol and Carlos found spoke perfectly of their union.

My friend's mother meant well; she wanted her daughter to get the most valuable car regardless of whether it came in the perfect color. But my friend's point was that if she was going to spend thousands of dollars on a new vehicle, she was determined to get just the one she wanted—color and all.

The same is true for finding the right wedding officiant: you have to respect the ideals of the person who is performing the ceremony, but don't settle for someone who doesn't match your genuine feelings for each other and for marriage. Your wedding day is one of the most important days of your life. Just as you wouldn't settle on a spouse, so should you not settle on wedding vows that don't reflect how you truly feel.

Your officiant may raise faith-based objections to your vows that will need to be considered and edited before the big day. But even those officiants who subscribe to the most traditional beliefs of their denomination will often allow for creative additions the couple would like to include in certain areas of the ceremony. Being open and honest with the officiant from the get-go will help you take ownership of your wedding ceremony, from the bridal march to the first kiss.

 Nuptial Nuggets

> If you think one of your loved ones would make the perfect officiant for your wedding but the person isn't certified to perform the ceremony, take heart: through the Universal Life Church, your friend or family member can become ordained and legally preside over your nuptials! (Check the laws in your state for specifics.) For more details, log on to www.ulc.net.

When Carl and Nancy were married in 1967, it was unheard of to alter the wedding vows they were instructed to use by the officiant.

"Vows out of the church framework would have been considered blasphemous, at the very least, and actually worthy of being thrown out of the church," Nancy says.

Some religious officiants still adhere to this strict interpretation of the wedding vow, but others have changed with the times, as more and more couples question the officiant on certain words they'd like to use—or avoid.

Nuptial Nuggets

In an age where second and third marriages are increasingly common, more and more brides and grooms are wary of traditional vows that include such phrases as "till death do us part." Some officiants allow the couple to change the wording to "as long as love shall last," but others say the expression of absolute faith in one's spouse and one's love is what makes the original wording so perfectly suited to a wedding vow.

Aside from all this talk of what officiants may and may not allow, you should think of the wedding officiant as a friend, not an enemy. A typical officiant has performed hundreds of ceremonies and is a wealth of information when it comes to great Bible verses, lovely quotes, and poems he has heard couples use over the years.

The officiant for my wedding was a local judge and family friend. Having performed countless wedding ceremonies before for people of all religious and ethnic backgrounds, he had a slew of ideas and examples from other nuptials we were able to use in our own wedding.

Begin Early

The earlier you start thinking about your wedding vows, the more time you have to find just the right words with which to say "I do." Before you even set a date and find a reception hall, you should be thinking about your wedding ceremony. For Laura, a newlywed, this thought process started way before she got engaged—or even met her spouse!

"I knew I wanted to say the traditional vows because I had heard those words recited so many times between so many beautiful couples," Laura says. "I remember going to my cousin Shelley's wedding at the age of 11 or so and hearing her and her husband-to-be Gary say the traditional vows, and thinking how cool would it be to have someone 'to have and to hold.'"

A decade later, when she met her husband, Curt, she knew she wanted to say those specific words to him. "Knowing we were reciting the same vows couples across the world have been reciting for so many years felt really special," she says, "like we were following the same path as so many people in love."

Laura is unique in that she contemplated her wedding vows years before she walked down the aisle. For many couples, the wedding vows seem to be the last thing on their minds. And because they're an afterthought, couples end up saying whatever the officiant tells them to, whether it suits them or not.

Basic Ceremony Elements

The first step to planning your wedding vows is to piece together the framework of your entire wedding ceremony. Do you want to include any readings, prayers, or songs? Will there be a sermon? What about an exchanging of rings or other gifts? If so, what will be said during that exchange?

Start paying attention at weddings you attend, or even ones you see on TV or in the movies. Which elements of the ceremony do you find touching? Which ones could you do without? For many, attending wedding ceremonies and receptions take on a whole new importance when you are planning your own nuptials. Remember, it's okay to steal ideas from other couples—in fact, it can be quite flattering!

Completing an outline for your wedding helps in more than one way. It gets both of you thinking about the real reason behind all this wedding day fuss. It also gives you an idea for what will be said during the rest of the ceremony and what sentiments will be saved for the actual exchanging of vows.

Nuptial Nuggets

In many countries, gifts are given to honor the parents of both bride and groom as part of the marriage celebration. I attended a friend's wedding a few months before mine in which the bride and groom took a few moments in the middle of the ceremony to leave the altar and give both of their mothers and grandmothers a single rose and a grateful hug. It was a touching moment that I chose to incorporate in my nuptials as well.

Most Christian wedding ceremonies follow the same basic outline:

1. Processional of wedding party

2. Opening remarks by officiant

3. The "giving away" of the bride (This is typically done by the bride's father or a father figure, who walks her up the aisle.)

4. Declaration of Intention (Also called Question of Intent or Declaration of Consent, this is where the officiant asks both bride and groom if they have come willingly to be married to the other, to love, honor, and cherish their spouse, to which the typical response is "I do" or "I will.")

5. Exchange of vows

6. Readings and rituals

7. Ring presentation/exchange
8. Blessings/closing remarks
9. Pronouncement of couple
10. Recessional

Sometimes a homily or sermon is included in the service, and other elements—such as the lighting of a *unity candle*—are inserted into the proceedings. Still other Christian denominations include a full Mass, with Communion, during the wedding.

Language of Love

The **unity candle** ceremony became popular in the 1990s. The bride and groom light two individual taper candles (or sometimes members of their families light the tapers) and then the bride and groom use those tapers to light one larger candle, a symbol of two lives becoming one. Some couples choose to blow out their individual tapers afterward, while others opt to keep those flames burning as well.

The Jewish wedding ceremony has two parts, both of which typically happen one right after the other:

1. The ketubah (marriage contract) is signed by both parties and at least two male witnesses.

2. Bedeken ("veiling of the bride"). Symbolizes the level of modesty a new bride should adhere to.

3. Processional to the chuppah.

4. Hakafot ("circling" of the groom). The bride circles the groom three or seven times, depending on custom, which some say symbolizes the protective wall the woman creates around her husband.

5. Welcome.

6. Two blessings given: Kiddush and Birkat Erusin.

7. Sharing common cup of wine.

8. Exchange of rings.

9. Ketubah read aloud.

10. Rabbi speaks.

11. *Sheva brachot* (seven blessings).

12. Bride and groom share the cup again.

13. Pronouncement and benediction.

14. Breaking of the glass—*Mazel tov!*

Muslim weddings are considered mostly legal affairs, after which there is much celebration:

1. The groom is asked for his consent to marriage.

2. The bride is asked—three times—for her consent.

3. The groom reads from the Koran.

4. Everyone agrees.

5. Imam declares them to be married.

6. The couple signs the wedding contract.

Although there are variations to each of these wedding ceremony outlines, knowing the basics will give you a head-start on planning your dream wedding.

Once you get the basic framework of your ceremony in place, you can start to think about what specifically will be said during each unique element. Contemplate what should be said during the exchanging of rings. Couples often consider this moment part of their wedding vows, and the words said at this time should also be a reflection of your commitment.

Also think about which, if any, readings of poetry, religious passages, or quotes you'd like to include in your ceremony. (See Chapter 6 for some suggestions.) Each of these elements should speak to the unique bond you're making. Although the actual wedding vows may only be a few sentences, you can use your entire wedding ceremony as an extended version of those vows.

Avoiding Déjà-Vu Vows: Let's Not Be Redundant

As you prepare your wedding vows, try to do more than merely reiterate the sentiments expressed in the rest of your ceremony.

Cynthia and Thomas initially told their officiant they were content with using the church's traditional vows. But then they were given a script of the entire traditional ceremony. Reading through it, they realized that promises to love, honor, cherish, and remain faithful were clearly spelled out not only in the vows, but in the Declaration of Intent and the wording used for the exchange of rings as well.

The more they thought about it, the more they realized that there was so much more they wanted to say! So they amended the script to include personally written vows they felt more thoroughly described their unique love story.

You want your vows to be the ultimate statement of love and commitment. You want them to be able to stand alone, apart from all the other traditions and rituals and prayers. They are, after all, meant to stand the test of time.

The Least You Need to Know

- Be aware of any religious requirements or ceremony site limitations and rules your wedding ceremony and vows need to adhere to.
- Choose a wedding officiant who complements your religious beliefs and respects your wedding day wishes.
- Be upfront with the wedding officiant about what you envision your wedding ceremony to be like as well as what you'd like to include in your vows.

- Start the planning process early so you and the officiant can work out any problems.

- Prepare an outline of the wedding ceremony before crafting your wedding vows.

A Couple Options: Personalizing Your Wedding Vows

In This Chapter

- Using traditional wedding vows
- Getting inspiration from wedding vows from around the world
- Altering traditional wedding vows
- Writing original wedding vows

Now that you realize just how important your wedding vows are, you may be feeling over-whelmed by the thought of finding just the right words to convey how you feel about your future spouse.

The beautiful thing about weddings—and wedding vows—is that thousands of couples have already walked down that aisle ahead of you. Using the most profound or the simplest words, they've pledged their lives and their love to each other. So there's no need to reinvent the wheel if you don't want to.

That said, the trick to figuring out what's right for your wedding vows is to take a look at several options. In this chapter, I give you some examples for traditional vows. I also explain how many couples alter traditional vows slightly to suit their beliefs and preferences. Finally, I offer some samples of unique vows written by couples who chose to break from tradition altogether.

Tried and True: Using Traditional Vows

Although your relationship is truly unique, the words you use on your wedding day don't necessarily have to be. Brides and grooms have uttered the very same words for generations because, quite simply, many of the world's traditional wedding vows are beautiful and timeless.

When Emily and Janet decided to hold a commitment ceremony to celebrate their lifelong bond to each other, they were torn about what kind of vows to use. Emily thought using the traditional vows would seem out of place because of the nontraditional nature of their relationship, but Janet had always wanted to look her life partner in the eye and promise "to love and to cherish, till death do us part," the same way she'd seen her siblings and friends do with their spouses. For her, the act of saying those exact words was far more important than knowing who traditionally says them.

After much debate, Janet was able to convince Emily that whether they said the traditional vows or wrote them from scratch, the words they used on their wedding day would be unique because of *who* was saying them.

The same is true for all couples. No matter how many thousands of times those famous words have been uttered, each time "I do" is said, it's special to the couple.

Traditional Religious Vows

When Ashley and Matt got engaged, the first thing they did was sit down with their pastor and discuss the specifics of the ceremony. They'd planned to write and memorize their own wedding vows, but as the pastor spoke about how weighty the actual wedding vows were, Ashley and Matt began to have second thoughts.

How could two nonwriters find the right words to express such deep emotion and everlasting commitment? The task they'd always daydreamed about suddenly felt like a challenge too overwhelming to meet. That's when they took another look at the traditional vows used in Ashley's parents' Episcopal Church and found just what they were looking for—in words they both basically knew by heart already.

The most traditional of all Christian vows are found in the "Form of Solemnization of Matrimony," from the Anglican Book of Common Prayer. The ceremony includes an exchanging of rings, during which the following is said by both bride and groom:

> With this Ring I thee wed, with my Body I thee worship, and with all my worldly Goods I thee endow; in the name of the Father, and of the Son, and of the Holy Ghost; Amen.

The actual vow exchange follows, both the groom and bride repeating virtually the same vows:

> I _____, take thee _____, to be my wedded wife/husband, to have and to hold from this day forward, for better, for worse, for richer, for poorer, in sickness and in health, to love and to cherish, till death us do part, according to God's holy ordinance; and thereto I plight thee my *troth*.

Language of Love

According to *Webster's New World College Dictionary*, **troth** means "faithfulness, loyalty, truth; one's pledged word or promise." The words *trust, true, troth,* and *betroth* are all related to the Old English word *treow*, which means "tree" and stands for the concepts of fidelity, faithfulness, and loyalty.

Here are the Roman Catholic Church's traditional wedding vows:

> I, _____, take you, _____, to be my wife/husband. I promise to be true to you in good times and in bad, in sickness and in health. I will love you and honor you all the days of my life.

And here are the vows used in the Presbyterian Church:

> I, _____, take thee _____, to be my wedded wife/husband, and I do promise and covenant, before God and these witnesses, to be thy loving and faithful wife/husband; in plenty and in want, in joy and in sorrow, in sickness and in health, as long as we both shall live.

And these are vows typically used in a Quaker wedding ceremony:

> In the presence of God and these our friends, I _____ take thee, _____, to be my husband/wife, promising with divine assistance to be unto thee a loving and faithful husband/ wife so long as we both shall live.

Traditional Secular Vows

There are several variations of traditional vows. The most basic nondenominational traditional wedding vows are the Question of Intention and the Standard Civil Ceremony.

The Question of Intention, which was adapted from the medieval Christian ceremony, begins with the officiant asking the couple to join hands before asking each—groom first—the following:

> _____, do you take _____ to be your wedded wife/husband to live together in marriage? Do you promise to love, comfort, honor, and keep her/him for better or worse, for richer or poorer, in sickness and in health and forsaking all others, be faithful only to her/him so long as you both shall live?

This question is, of course, answered by "I do."

In the Standard Civil Ceremony, the bride and groom make similar statements for themselves rather than answering questions:

> _____, I take you to be my lawfully wedded wife/husband. Before these witnesses I vow to love you and care for you as long as we both shall live. I take you, with all of your faults and strengths, as I offer myself to you with my faults and strengths. I will help you when you need help, and will turn to you when I need help. I choose you as the person with whom I will spend my life.

Other Traditions from World Religions and Cultures

As I stated in the beginning of this chapter, the institution of marriage is universal, but the details of the wedding ceremony, and the vows themselves, can differ greatly from country to country, continent to continent.

Learning about the different ways couples tie the knot in faraway countries can help you as you think about your own wedding vows and what they should include.

Perhaps you want to honor your family's heritage by incorporating a time-honored tradition from your ancestors' homeland. Or you'd just like to think outside the box to add some international flavor to your one-of-a-kind nuptials. For hundreds of years, men and women from Mexico to Malaysia have been saying "I do" in ways from the sentimental to the silly.

Greek Orthodox Tradition

Couples getting married in the Greek Orthodox Church don't have the stress of writing, memorizing, or even repeating their own wedding vows. In fact, they don't say anything at all. In Greek Orthodox tradition, showing up to the wedding ceremony itself proves the couple's willingness to commit to each other and to accept God into their lives. The bride and groom exchange rings, don crowns, walk around the altar, and drink from a common cup. But they don't utter a word.

Mexican Wedding Tradition

A Mexican bride gets a little more than just a husband on her wedding day. During the wedding ceremony, her groom gives her 13 gold coins (*arras*), which are first blessed by the priest. The number of coins represents Christ and his 12 disciples. The gift is a sign of the groom's trust and confidence in his bride, as well as a symbol of giving her his fortune to support her.

The bride's acceptance of the coins symbolizes that she will keep the groom's trust unconditionally. The tradition originated in Spain and is also upheld in several other countries, including the Philippines.

Wedding Tradition in Iran

At a wedding in Iran, the wedding officiant asks for the groom's consent to enter into marriage, to which he says yes. Then the officiant asks for the bride's consent, and there is silence. He asks three times before the bride answers. The delay signifies that it's the husband who seeks the wife and not the other way around. Once the bride says yes, the officiant declares them husband and wife. Then they exchange rings and feed each other honey to start their sweet life together.

Japanese Sake Tradition

In a Shinto Japanese wedding ceremony, while the bride and groom exchange their vows, their two families face each other instead of the couple in a symbolic joining of the families.

The bride and groom also perform the *San-san-kudo* exchange of nuptial cups. *San-san-kudo* means

$3 \times 3 = 9$, and the three cups are each brought to the lips three times, with one sip of sake each time. The number three is significant in Japan, so there are three cups, the sake is poured three times, and three sips are taken from each cup.

African American Wedding Tradition

A wedding tradition among African Americans is to "jump the broom." It's pretty much what it sounds like: a decorated broom is placed on the floor and the couple jumps over it. The tradition is said to have originated in the South during times of slavery, when slaves were largely forbidden to marry. So they came up with this tradition to signify a couple's matrimonial union instead. Jumping the broom has been linked to the Celts as well.

Celtic Wedding Vows

Here is a sampling of traditional Celtic vows:

> I vow to you the first cut of my meat, the first sip of my wine, from this day on it shall be only your name I cry out in the night and into your eyes that I smile each morning; I shall be a shield for your back as you are for mine, nor shall a grievous word be spoken about us, for our marriage is sacred between us and no stranger shall hear my grievance. Above and beyond this, I will cherish and honor you through this life and into the next. Ye are blood of my blood, and bone of my bone. I give ye my body, that we two might be one. I give ye my spirit, till our life shall be done.

New Word Order: Making a Few Changes

Sometimes the traditional wedding vows seem almost right, but not quite. For example, in the vows taken from the Anglican Book of Common Prayer, the man promises "to love and to cherish," while the woman pledges "to love, cherish, and obey." Many modern ceremonies amend these vows, usually taking out "obey" and making both vows identical.

Altering Traditional Christian Vows

Michelle had a different problem with the traditional vows spoken in her church. She and her husband, Tim, used, as she put it, the "old standard" wedding vows because Tim was too bashful to write and deliver his own. Knowing and loving Tim for who he was, this wasn't a problem for Michelle. But when she took a look at the vows given to her by her pastor, she was uncomfortable saying one particular phrase.

"The only change I had to our vows was the 'till death do you part' phrase," Michelle says. "I hated that reference to death, so I changed it to 'till the Lord calls us home.' It just sounded nicer."

Like Michelle, my husband, Christopher, also didn't like the mention of death in our wedding vows. But he had a different reason for tweaking that last line.

"Saying 'till death do us part' makes it sound like my love and honor for my bride will end when one of us dies," he says. "But I know I'll be committed to her forever, from this life to the next."

Who could argue with such a romantic? Our wedding vows were shortened from "till death do us part" to "forever."

Nuptial Nuggets

In the Catholic Church, the bride and groom technically are the ministers of their own union and have more freedom when choosing the wording of their vows than some might imagine. The priest is there to sanctify the marriage, not create it. So when a Catholic couple says "Father John married us," they mean in a legal sense. In actuality, they married themselves!

Altering Civil Ceremony Vows

Some couples like the sentiments in the traditional vows but don't want them to sound so formal. Even the standard civil ceremony vows can be amended to take out "before these witnesses" or add the ever-popular "for richer, for poorer, in sickness and in health." Other couples like to shorten the traditional ring exchange vow to the more succinct "With this ring, I thee wed."

Betsy and Gregg, an interfaith couple, wrote their civil ceremony themselves. They meshed elements from several traditional wedding vows into one that sounded just right for them:

> I, Betsy, take you, Gregg, to be my lawfully wedded husband, to love and to cherish, from this day forward, for better, for worse, in sickness and in health, in joy and in sorrow, all the days of my life.

Two friends who were not very religious but believed in God chose to use most of the elements from the standard civil ceremony. However, they wanted to acknowledge their spirituality, so they added a simple phrase to their vows:

> Before God and these witnesses, I vow to love you and care for you as long as we both shall live. I take you, with all of your faults and strengths, as I offer myself to you with all my faults and strengths. I will help you when you need help and will turn to you when I need help. I choose you as the person with whom I will spend my life.

Altering the Jewish Ketubah

Using the text of a traditional ketubah speaks to the importance of Jewish tradition and community. But today some couples opt to amend the ketubah, adding their own words to the original to keep the tradition of so many couples before them, while at the same time finding a way to express their unique union.

Nuptial Nuggets

If you want to alter the ketubah but your family or rabbi prefers that you use the traditional text in your wedding ceremony, you can always create a second ketubah just for the two of you to hang in your home. Make it as simple or elaborate as you want, including everything you want to say to each other. If you can't work it into the ceremony itself, be sure to set aside some quiet time sometime on your wedding day to read it together.

Here's one example of a ketubah altered for an interfaith couple:

> Standing under the chuppah they said to each other: As beloveds and friends we choose to walk life's path together. We pledge to be equal partners, loving friends, and supportive companions all through our life. May our love provide us with the freedom to be ourselves and the courage to follow our mutual and individual paths. As we share life's experiences, we vow to create an intimacy that will enable us to express our innermost thoughts and feelings;

to be sensitive to each other's needs; to share life's joys; to comfort each other through life's sorrows; to challenge each other to achieve intellectual and physical fulfillment as well as spiritual and emotional tranquility. We will build a home together and fill it with laughter, empathy, faith, imagination, trust, friendship, companionship, and love; a home in which holidays and heritage are celebrated in accordance with Jewish culture and tradition, and respect is fostered for the cultures of both our families. May we live each day as the first, the last, the only day we will have with each other. We joyfully enter into this covenant and solemnly accept the obligations herein.

Points for Originality

As beautiful as traditional wedding vows are, sometimes couples feel the need to express their love in a truly original way. When Rungsee and Nancy got married, Rungsee, a Buddhist, knew that any form of the traditional wedding vows just wasn't for him, and he enjoyed the challenge of finding just the right words to define his love for Nancy.

"It was really fun writing my vows," Rungsee says. "At first, I started going through different song lyrics and poems. I was this close to using the lyrics from a Dave Matthews Band song. But I remember reading them over and over and thinking, *You know what, it would mean more if I wrote them myself.* So I did."

For Rungsee, conveying his love and devotion for Nancy couldn't be done using someone else's words because what he wanted to tell her seemed to break from the mold of what most brides and grooms focus on in their wedding vows.

"Everyone writes about the happy times, but I wanted to write something that showed how I would be there for not-so-happy times, too," Rungsee says. "After all, that I believe is one of the most important parts of marriage."

Rungsee's original wedding vows to Nancy were a reflection of just what he thought marriage should be:

> For the one who makes me laugh,
> I will comfort you when you cry.
> For the one who brightens my days,
> I will hold you when you are down.
> For the one who truly believes in me,
> I will always be by your side.
> And for the one who shares her life with me,
> I will love you with all my heart.

When Kielynn-Marie married Luis, she wanted her wedding vows to be special in two ways. First, she wished to convey to her groom just how happy she was to have found her perfect mate. Second, she wanted to tell him how she felt using Spanish, his native language.

Nuptial Nuggets

Some brides and grooms can't decide on a wedding cake flavor so they serve two! The same idea can be applied to the wedding vows. If you and your future spouse just can't decide between using traditional vows and writing your own, ask your wedding officiant if you can do both! You may be able to say a few words of your own to each other before going ahead with the traditional vows.

So writing her wedding vows became twice as challenging. She first chose the feelings she wanted to express and then had a friend help translate it into Spanish, changing a few phrases to make it sound as poetic as she thought a wedding vow should:

> *Luis, le pedí a Dios por ti. Antes de conocerte. Aun antes de saber de tu existencia, le pedí a Dios por ti. Le pedí a Dios que me enviara un hombre con honor. Le pedí a Dios que me enviara un hombre compasivo. Un hombre con fortaleza. Le pedí a Dios que me enviara al padre de mis hijos.*

> *Todo lo que tengo, todo lo que quiero, y todo lo que necesito, lo encuentro cuando te veo a los ojos. Y sé que Dios ha escuchado mis oraciones y me ha bendecido contigo.*

The English translation is just as beautiful:

> Luis, I asked God for you. Before I knew you. Before I even knew you existed, I asked God for you. I asked God to send me a man with honor. I asked God to send me a compassionate man, a man with strength. I asked God to send me the father of my children.
>
> All that I have, all that I want, and all that I need, I see when I look in your eyes. And I know that God has listened to my prayers and has blessed me with you.

Learning to say the vows in Spanish took plenty of practice, but Kielynn-Marie says seeing Luis' eyes light up as she began speaking Spanish to him on his wedding day made all her extra efforts worthwhile.

 Word to the Wise

> If you'd like to incorporate wedding vows or other elements of your wedding ceremony in a language other than what is spoken by the majority of those attending, be sure the translation of your special vows is listed in the wedding program or translated for your guests during the ceremony. That way, everyone feels included and can share in the beauty of the promises you're making to each other.

Kielynn-Marie wrote her vows by thinking of all the ways her husband-to-be was the answer to her prayers. Sometimes original vows express what your spouse means to you. Sometimes they express what you promise to be to them:

> I vow to be the rock upon which you stand, so you can be sure nothing will harm you or side-track you from your dreams. I vow to catch you when you fall, and to lift you when you can't quite reach. I will be the smile you seek after a hard day, the comforting shoulder you need in a time of sorrow, and the dream that helps you sleep peacefully each night.

Still other couples focus on the life the two of them will lead, starting from the moment they walk back down the aisle, as husband and wife:

> Today I stand with you on the threshold of a new life, a better life, for we will be united as one. From this day forward your burdens are my burdens, your joys are my joys, and your happiness is my greatest dream. I look forward to walking with you, hand in hand, over every obstacle that life places before us. The challenges of life get easier today, and the joys of life get sweeter, because I no longer face them alone.
>
> With a heart full of joy I look down that aisle and envision our life together, filled with laughter and love and beauty. Yours is the hand

I will hold as we climb every obstacle, admire every view, rejoice in every accomplishment. Everything I have and all that I am I share with you. I know that our lives will be doubly blessed and our dreams twice as sweet because I am yours, and you are mine—today, tomorrow and always.

There are vows about what you will do, and vows about what you won't do:

I will spend each day truly living the moments with you, and each night dreaming of our tomorrows. I will honor you in thought, word, and deed. I will strive to be the person you can be proud to call yours. From this day forward, I will always find goodness in the world, simply because you are in it.

I will never again fear the future, for you are by my side. I will not seek companionship outside our home, for it is you who warms my heart. And I will not lose sight of your dreams, for they are now my own.

Some vows focus on the good times; others on the bad times. But as long as they're focused on the love you have for each other, you're sure to have a wonderful wedding day.

The Least You Need to Know

- Many traditional wedding vows are simple, poetic, and timeless.

- Wedding traditions and vows of religions and cultures around the world can serve as inspiration for your own nuptials.

- Sometimes altering just a few words or phrases in a traditional wedding vow creates the perfect promise for your nuptials.

- Writing original wedding vows allows you to express exactly what you want to share with your beloved in your own unique way.

Chapter 5

Pen Pals: Working With Your Partner

In This Chapter

- Thinking about what marriage means
- Keeping your audience in mind
- Knowing what you want to hear

You've read all about what wedding vows are and how much they mean. You've perused the traditional vows and the not-so-traditional ones. And you've decided to give writing your own vows a shot. This decision may seem like the only one you need to make, but in actuality, it opens up a whole host of other questions you'll need to answer.

Will you write one vow together and both recite it? Or do you want to each write your own personal statements for your significant other? Will your vows be in poem form? What will they include? And will you read your vows to each other before your wedding day?

It takes two people to answer all these questions. In this chapter, I help you work together to be sure you're on the same page with this vow-writing challenge—not to mention your upcoming marriage.

Assessing Your Relationship

The ring is on her finger, and the tuxes have been ordered. That doesn't mean it's too late to think about—and talk about—your relationship. In fact, it's the perfect time!

Because you're swimming in wedding details and basking in the engagement glow, your minds and hearts are in the right positions to think seriously about what it is you're about to do.

But before you sit down together, you should each take some quiet time alone to reflect on who you are individually and who you are—and would like to be—as a couple.

Meditate for a bit on your life, your love, and your future. It sounds heavy, but it should be relaxing, not stressful. Think about the happy times, and think about the times that weren't happy but were made more bearable because of your partner's presence or assistance.

Word to the Wise _____

> To get in to the right frame of mind to write your vows and discuss marriage with your spouse, spend some quiet time going through old photographs of the two of you. Sort through old letters and birthday cards or re-read saved e-mails from your beloved. Reflecting on your past, most especially the happy times and holidays, the parties and laughter, and the milestones, will have your creative juices flowing in no time.

To help you focus, each of you could spend a while pondering these questions:

- How did you meet? What were your first impressions?
- How have those first impressions changed, if at all?
- What was your first kiss like? Where and how did it happen?
- Describe your beloved. Be as descriptive as possible.
- List a few of the reasons you love your partner.
- What are some special moments and memories you've shared, both happy and sad? How, if at all, did they change the way you viewed your partner?

- When did you know he/she was "the one"? Was there a moment? A gut feeling? Did it happen quickly or gradually?

- What are some of the things your partner says to you or does for you that you love?

- What are some of the things your partner says to you or does for you that you don't like?

- What was the engagement like? What's the first thing you remember when you think of it? How did you feel?

- Why are you marrying this person?

- How do you want to be treated in a marriage?

- How do you plan to treat your spouse?

- How do you think your life will change when you are married?

 Word to the Wise

Grab some paper or a journal and write the answers to these questions, or just write your thoughts about your future spouse.

Not only could this end up being a sweet entry in a wedding scrapbook, but in jotting down your thoughts about your spouse, you could unwittingly be writing some tidbits you'll later use to form your wedding vows.

You don't have to answer all these questions, but doing so will help get you focused on your future spouse—which is the frame of mind you need to write the perfect wedding vows for that person.

Writing Vows Together

For many couples, the idea of writing their own wedding vows conjures up an image of two people scribbling secret notes in separate rooms, coming up with something to surprise their significant other with on their wedding day.

Although there's nothing wrong with wanting to wait until you're at the altar to share your vows with each other, don't write your vows separately without at least some sort of discussion first. There's a reason why these are called "wedding vows": there's more than one! Even if you and your spouse recite the same vow, two pledges are being made. Write or at least consider your vows together.

What Does Marriage Mean?

After you've both spent some time separately thinking about your past, present, and future as a couple, set aside some more time to sit and talk about your relationship.

It may sound obvious, but it's important to be sure you both understand how the other is viewing your future nuptials.

Many couples talk about marriage before they get engaged, but it's usually in the abstract sense: "When we're married, we'll buy a house and get a dog and take romantic weekend getaway trips together." These little fantasies are nice, and may very well come true, but there's much more to marriage than planning exotic trips and dreaming up names for your future babies.

Everyone has his or her own sense of what marriage is, and many couples don't ever sit down and discuss those perceptions. They assume their significant other wants and expects the same things out of the marriage as they do.

But it doesn't hurt to ask. When you're standing up at that altar, looking into the eyes of the person to whom you're pledging the rest of your life, you want the words you're saying to be as meaningful to that person as they are to you.

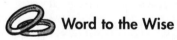 **Word to the Wise**

> You don't have to spend hours ruminating about your relationship to be sure you're on the same page. To simplify the process, ask each other to define the following words: *love, marriage, commitment,* and *family.* Your partner's answers should only pleasantly surprise you!

Talking about your marriage will keep you and your beloved on the same page as you plan to join your futures together. But it also has the added benefit of getting you in the right frame of mind to begin writing your vows.

Find some quiet time when you're both in the mood to discuss wedding plans, and instead of talking about the caterer or the wedding favors, talk about the marriage itself.

You can use the following questions as a guide, or just try to express to your significant other what you think it is you'll really be doing when you walk down that aisle and say "I do."

- What makes a marriage?
- Why do you want to get married?
- What are you hoping our marriage will be like?
- What are you expecting from me as your spouse?
- Are there any things in your life as a single person you don't want to give up or change once we're married?
- What do you think was the most important event in our relationship so far, and how did it change us?
- Do you have visions of us pursuing any particular hobbies, goals, or dreams together?

You don't have to sit down with this list of questions and a piece of paper and answer them all in essay form. Just try to put into words what you both want your future to be like. It will hopefully open up a dialogue that could be the most important conversation you have before your wedding day.

 Word to the Wise _____

> Sometimes promising "forever" seems too daunting a task. One might think, *I love this person with all my heart today, but what about 20 years from now?* The trick is to take that promise and make it into a thousand small promises, to wake up each morning and re-commit yourself to your spouse. Life is not lived in the future, after all. It is lived in the present. So when you promise today and then get up and make the same unspoken commitment the next day, and the next day, and the next ... "today" really does become "forever."

I have seen couples who wrote their vows separately, and when they said them to each other on their wedding day, it was clear to everyone witnessing the nuptials that they had different visions of what was most important in the union they were creating.

If you choose to write two wedding vows, it's natural for the two vows to sound distinct; they're being written and expressed by two unique individuals. But the underlying themes in those vows should probably mirror each other, because that means those two individuals know they are headed down the same path.

To stay relatively on the same page but give each other plenty of creative freedom, consider crafting your individual vows around an agreed-upon theme. That's what Javier and Ana did. The couple, both avid skiers, met on a mountain where Javier was an instructor and Ana was skiing with friends. Both are free spirits, so they chose to write their own wedding vows but wanted each one to echo the sentiments of the other. They agreed to use the mountain as the theme of their vows, which made them even more personal and poignant:

> Ana, when I look at you I am reminded of the day we met. Until that moment, I thought the mountain we were standing on was the most breathtaking sight in the world. Now I see that mountain in my dreams, for it is where my life changed in the first flash of your smile. I will live each day to see that smile, will work to make you happy, safe, honored and loved, all the days of my life.

> Javier, we met on a beautiful snow-capped mountain (your charm captured me, even through that thick jacket and sunglasses), and three years later you have, in many ways,

become my mountain. Through you I see the
beauty of life, with you I am given greater
perspective, a sense of place in this world, and
true inner peace. The peaks and valleys of life
await us, and I face it all not with trepidation
but with joy and thankfulness. I will honor,
love, cherish, and laugh with you all the days
of my life.

If you don't have a natural common theme the way
Ana and Javier did, consider using a symbol that
already has some meaning to it, such as wedding
rings, music, water, wine, or light.

Keep Your Audience in Mind

The most basic rule to writing anything, from a
high school essay to a job resumé, is to keep your
audience in mind. This applies to writing wedding
vows as well. The only way to write clear, meaningful wedding vows is to take a good look at who
you're marrying—not just his or her physical
makeup, but his whole being. What makes him
tick? What does she need to feel safe, happy, and
loved?

Now, what can you do to accomplish that? And
how can you tell your soon-to-be that you will?

Bob, a Christian minister, knew his beloved, Rita,
was happiest when he took time out of his busy day
to spend with her. With a job like his, for which his
time was often spent tending to others' needs, he
knew it was necessary to spell out how he would

work to fulfill his wife's natural need for companionship. So he promised to tithe his time to her, dedicating at least 10 percent of each and every day to his wife. He even kept a small notebook documenting the time they spent together to prove he was serious about this vow.

Nuptial Nuggets _____

For fun, create mock wedding vows that include some of the silly little things you love about your spouse or are willing to do for them. During the wedding rehearsal, when the officiant gets to the part where you exchange vows, you can "exchange" these vows to lighten the mood and entertain your partner and your wedding party. You can also write a set of wedding vows that are a little more risqué than the usual "love, honor, and cherish." But save those vows for the honeymoon!

Besides figuring out what your spouse wants and needs from you out of marriage, you also should keep in mind what kinds of words, phrases, and promises will speak to them loudest.

If your boyfriend is a man of simple words, don't write an elaborate sonnet. If your fiancé is a hopeless romantic, try your hand at a few meaty *metaphors* or *similes*. You have to find the right balance: you want the formality of the language to be somewhere between a formal letter and a note scribbled to your beloved and left on the kitchen table.

Language of Love

A **metaphor** is a figure of speech in which a word is applied to an object or action as a symbol, not as its true meaning. For example, "my love for you is an endless ocean," or "this ring is my promise to you," are metaphors. A **simile** is a figure of speech used to compare two things using the word *like:* "You are like the full moon on a cloudless night" and "My love is like a rose" are similes.

Above all, don't overthink it. You don't want your vows so flowery they sound like you're committing yourself to a queen or to Shakespeare himself. You want your vows to come from the heart, but you want them to speak directly to your beloved's heart—not to read like they were ripped from the pages of a romance novel. Unless, of course, she likes romance novels …

Word to the Wise

Although your main audience for this bit of writing is your future spouse, keep in mind that your partner is not the only one who's going to hear what you have to say. The vows are a public pledge, so even though they should not be looked at as some kind of performance, they're also not the right venue for inside jokes or references to very personal business. Your vows should be personal without invading your beloved's privacy by mentioning things that should be kept to yourselves.

While studying your partner for what he or she needs and figuring out just how you should tell him or her what it is you want to say, you must also recognize the challenges your significant other may be facing by agreeing to write wedding vows to you.

Let's face it: some people are writers; some are poets; some are hopeless romantics. But many, many others are just ... not. These are not bad people or in any way inadequate. There are lots of ways to say, "I love you," and everyone, writer or not, seems to find a way.

For instance, Owen always keeps gas in Grace's car. He doesn't pen long love letters to his wife. Instead, he shows her he loves her with simple gestures like filling up her gas tank so she's never stranded. That's a gesture of love.

There are a thousand such gestures in a million different relationships, and all of them are special.

Sometimes a person who feels in tune to their romantic side wants to write original wedding vows while their partner doesn't feel qualified to do so. But it's important for these nonpoets in the crowd to realize that they, too, probably do have a romantic side. They just haven't labeled it so.

They may think they'll have a harder time with the challenge of writing their vows, but they're actually ahead of the game. After all, simple romantic gestures like Owen filling Grace's gas tank take an intimate understanding and awareness of one's partner and what's important to them— what makes them happy. Clearly, Owen knows what makes Grace feel safe, happy, and loved. And if he puts his mind to it, he can translate that knowledge into words.

The bottom line is that nobody should be intimidated by this vow-writing task. The vows you're writing are for the same person in front of whom you have probably made a fool of yourself at least once. They've seen you at your best and at your worst. And they already love you, "for better or for worse," no matter how you word your wedding vows.

Word to the Wise

Have the perfect vow jumbled up in your head, but can't seem to get it in writing? You might have writer's block. Get up from your chair and go do something else for a while. Get a snack, take a walk, talk to a friend, or do whatever you can to clear your mind. Then return to the task at hand when you feel a little fresher. Also, if you've been trying to type your vows into a computer, grab a pen and paper and write that way for a while.

What Do *You* Want to Hear?

It might seem silly, but your significant other isn't the only one you should be concentrating on while writing your vows, or even thinking about writing them. You should also think about you.

What are your needs? What are your desires for marriage—both secret and not so secret? What is it that you want to hear your partner say to you on your wedding day?

I'm not saying you should make a list of demands or create unrealistic expectations in your head that will leave you disappointed by what you do or don't hear your beloved say to you. I'm talking about knowing what you want your spouse to be for you. Writing—and hearing—the perfect wedding vows for you is dependent upon you both knowing what it is you want, expect, and hope from each other.

Do you need your future spouse to be supportive of your career? Are you most hoping for a loving parent to your children? Do you see yourself as the main provider, or do you hope to be supported financially by your partner? You'd be surprised how many couples don't voice such expectations before they say "I do."

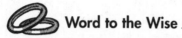 **Word to the Wise** _____

> In his book *Men Are from Mars, Women Are from Venus,* John Gray points out that men and women want and need different things out of a relationship. He says men are more likely to want to be trusted, appreciated, and accepted for who they are. Women are more likely to want to be supported, cared for, and respected. Keep these differences in mind when writing your wedding vows.

Think about the vows you've read in this book, as well as any others you've read or heard at weddings before. Which words or ideas particularly touched your heart? These are probably things you want to hear your significant other address as well.

Think about the good and the bad—not in your relationship, but in life. Think about what you will do when times are rough, and what you hope your spouse will do for you in those tough times as well.

Wish List Exercise

I'm sure the hopeless romantic inside you wants your significant other just to speak from the heart and write whatever vows he or she is inspired to write. But I'm here to tell you that it's a good idea to let poor Romeo know if there's something specific you're hoping to hear—and I'm also here to tell you that there probably is.

So before you retreat to separate rooms to begin writing your wedding day masterpieces, make a wish list of what you're hoping will be included in your vows and then compare lists.

Here are some examples to get you wishing and listing:

- Are you hoping to hear your partner tell you what you have meant to them?

- Do you want to hear promises for what tomorrow will bring with your future spouse?

- Are you envisioning your wedding vows to be poetic?

- How long do you think the wedding vows should be?

- Would you like to hear the same words spoken by your partner that you will speak to them?

- Do you want God to be a part of your wedding vows?

- Are you hoping your partner will mention family—either your extended family or the family you may one day have together?

Really knowing who you are, and who you're marrying, makes writing your wedding vows almost as much fun as it will be to deliver them. It is an honor and a joy to stand before someone you adore and see the love in your partner's eyes as he or she listens to the pledges you are making, straight from your heart.

The Least You Need to Know

- Whether you write your vows separately or not, you and your partner should consider a few things together first.

- Be sure you're on the same page about your expectations for married life.

- To get the creative juices flowing, spend some time thinking about your relationship so far and where you'd like to see it headed.

- Keep your audience in mind when writing your vows.

- Find out if your partner hopes to hear anything in particular in your vows, and let him know if you're hoping to hear anything specific from him.

Chapter 6

Words' Worth: Finding Your Inner Shakespeare

In This Chapter

- Choosing the right words
- Finding inspiration in others' words
- Adding a personal touch to your vows

It's time to put pen to paper and write your wedding vows, and you're still a little nervous. You might think you know what you want to say; you can feel it in your heart. But how do you translate a heartful of feelings into something that will be understood by both your beloved and the rest of your friends and family attending your wedding?

It's not as daunting as it might seem. After all, you've already done so much: you've thought about why your partner is the right one for you, you've contemplated what marriage to this person will be like, and you know what you will do to make him or her happy. So really, all that's left is to translate those sentiments into a few simple sentences.

Here is where vocabulary matters, where feelings are symbolized with words. In this chapter, I help you find just the right words to spell out your true love and your truest intentions for your marriage.

Why Vocabulary Matters

Words can move mountains—and hearts. So in this task you've set for yourself—writing your wedding vows—your dearest ally is a decent vocabulary. I'll spare you the grammar lesson, but I will offer you some assistance—or, at the very least, encouragement—with writing something as important as your wedding vows.

But first things first: you're not being graded. Unless she's a close personal friend, your high school English teacher will not be sitting in the back of the church noticing whether you've misplaced a modifier or ended a sentence with a dangling participle.

You and your fiancé will be looked at through kind eyes on your wedding day. The fact that you'll be up there in front of everyone publicly declaring your love will be enough to make every heart in attendance swoon, no matter what you say. So even if you're not entirely sure what a dangling participle is, cast out your fear and open your heart.

Paula really wanted her fiancé Peter to write his wedding vow to her, but frankly, he was frightened to do so. He'd been an okay student in high school but never mastered English class. His spelling was atrocious; even his handwriting was practically illegible.

But Paula's heart was set on the two of them exchanging original vows. So Peter gave it a shot. He sat down, thought about his beloved for a long time, and then picked up his pen and wrote a few simple sentences about her. When he was finished, he had written something he hadn't thought possible—a wedding vow:

> Paula, there is nothing in this world that makes me happier than when I'm with you. Your eyes are the sweetest eyes I have ever seen. Your hands are the warmest hands I have ever held. You are all I need in this life. I will do everything I can to keep you safe, happy, and loved.

Of course, Peter didn't think it was perfect at first. He thought it was too simple, too short, too boring. He wrote and rewrote, scratching out words and inserting others … until he glanced back at his original vow and realized that those were the words that came from his heart. And if his heart was good enough for Paula, then so were those words.

Peter did two important things: first, he wrote from his heart, keeping his audience in mind the whole time. Second, he stayed true to himself, the author. He did not try to emulate Emerson or sound like Shakespeare; if he had, his vow wouldn't have sounded half as original or sincere.

Word to the Wise

If you're not much of a writer and are trying to figure out what writing voice suits you best, head to your nearest Hallmark store and peruse the cards on love and marriage. Read a few dozen cards, and hold on to any that move you or sound like something you would say. Then study those cards in your hands. Are the messages long and flowery, full of vivid imagery and powerful prose? Or are they simply stated? This should give you an idea for the kind of language that matches your personality.

In "Journals," Emerson wrote, "A poem, a sentence, causes us to see ourselves. I be, and I see my being, at the same time."

Too often people think that their vows have to sound beautiful and poetic, so they concentrate on finding pretty words to fill up their sentences, instead of focusing on what it is they truly want to say.

When it comes to writing a wedding vow, don't lose sight of yourself. You should be aiming for clarity first and foremost. You are pledging your life to someone else—better be sure that fact is not buried beneath a heap of adjectives or exhausted by a string of run-on sentences.

Be simple, direct, and accurate. Don't write for the sake of writing; write for the sake of being understood.

With all that said, language that is beautiful and poignant can and should be utilized in your wedding vows. After all, you're portraying the deepest emotions and most honorable commitments you might ever have.

Parts of Speech

By the time we're adults, many of us write without thinking. We sign birthday cards, leave notes for loved ones, send e-mails and letters, all without paying too much attention to the words we use, beyond using the spell check function on the computer. We rarely worry which adjective is the exact one we mean, or whether we need an adverb to perfectly describe the act we're, well, describing.

But many couples want their wedding vows to be more descriptive. This is bigger than a "to-do" list, more permanent than an e-mail; this is a lifelong pledge.

When you're writing a mini-speech such as vows, it pays to be aware of the parts of speech you're using. Once you've boiled down your feelings to the most important points you want to make, look at the words you've used. Then, to be sure you're including everything you want to say, take a moment and brainstorm some words that come to mind when you think of your fiancé.

Verbs to Use

Study your notes and decide which actions you'd like to let your loved one know you are prepared to take and how you feel about him or her today. These are the verbs you should include in your vows.

To help get your creative juices flowing, these verbs could all work well in a wedding vow:

admire	hope	respect
adore	inspire	sacrifice
believe	keep	share
cherish	love	support
comfort	marvel	unite
commit	obey	uphold
cultivate	please	value
desire	pledge	vow
dream	promise	
honor	renew	

Nouns to Use

Next, think of the qualities your beloved brings out in you and in your relationship. These are the nouns you should try to include in your vows. Here are a few that are used in some of the most traditional vows:

affection	fear	love
bond	forever	loyalty
commitment	fulfillment	optimism
companionship	grace	peace
dedication	gratitude	respect
devotion	happiness	sincerity
eternity	harmony	truth
faith	honor	union
beauty	joy	wisdom

Adjectives to Use

Use adjectives to better describe the qualities you're including in your vows. Here are a few adjectives typically used with the nouns previously listed:

beautiful	happy	sincere
better	honest	tender
charming	hopeful	undying
content	loving	unique
endless	meaningful	vibrant
faithful	perfect	virtuous
fun	priceless	warm

Adverbs to Use

So how will you do what it is you're saying you'll do in this marriage? This is when adverbs should be used, to modify the verbs in your vows. A few to consider:

always	increasingly	sincerely
completely	magically	totally
faithfully	passionately	unbendingly
genuinely	respectfully	undoubtedly

Become a Collector

Famed public speaker Dale Carnegie once said, "The ideas I stand for are not mine. I borrowed them from Socrates. I swiped them from Chesterfield. I stole them from Jesus. And I put them in a book. If you don't like their rules, whose would you use?"

Writing your own wedding vows from scratch might be the way to go, but then again, Carnegie was onto something. When it comes to a clever turn of phrase or a striking metaphor, it's hard to top the authors of the Bible or playwright William Shakespeare.

When creating your own wedding vows, you don't just have the words in your heart at your disposal; you've got all the words ever written that you can get your hands on. Instead of pulling your hair out trying to come up with something as moving as

Shakespeare's Sonnet 18, "Shall I Compare Thee to a Summer's Day?" why not quote from the sonnet itself?

Word to the Wise

While you're reading the poems and passages of the world's greatest writers, keep in mind that you're not only creating your wedding vows, you're also planning an entire wedding ceremony and reception. Everything from the ceremony readings to the program to the wedding toast can be infused with a little prose from the literary greats who came before you!

So start searching. Find Bible passages that move you. Get inspired by poets such as Emily Dickinson; Alfred, Lord Tennyson; and John Keats. Pick up a book of romantic quotations, and discover a new perspective on marriage you hadn't thought of before but want to include in your wedding vows.

Reading the works of others can help you further focus on what it is you want to say. And sometimes you'll find that someone else has already said it, quite perfectly, before you.

Bible Verses

The Bible is a treasure-trove of passages about love, commitment, honor, and family. Quoting from Scripture in your wedding vows is an excellent way to incorporate God in the tenets of your marriage. Here are a few of the many Bible passages you could use in your vows and wedding readings:

1 Corinthians 13:4–13:

> Love is patient, love is kind. It does not envy, it does not boast, it is not proud. It is not rude, it is not self-seeking, it is not easily angered, it keeps no record of wrongs. Love does not delight in evil but rejoices with the truth. It always protects, always trusts, always hopes, always perseveres.

> Love never fails. But where there are prophecies, they will cease; where there are tongues, they will be stilled; where there is knowledge, it will pass away. For we know in part and we prophesy in part, but when perfection comes, the imperfect disappears. When I was a child, I talked like a child, I thought like a child, I reasoned like a child. When I became a man, I put childish ways behind me. Now we see but a poor reflection as in a mirror; then we shall see face to face. Now I know in part; then I shall know fully, even as I am fully known.

> And now these three remain: faith, hope and love. But the greatest of these is love.

John 15:12–14:

> My command is this: Love each other as I have
> loved you. Greater love has no one than this,
> that he lay down his life for his friends. You are
> my friends if you do what I command.

Ecclesiastes 4:9–12:

> Two are better than one, because they have a
> good return for their work; If one falls down,
> his friend can help him up. But pity the man
> who falls and has no one to help him up! Also,
> if two lie down together, they will keep warm.
> But how can one keep warm alone? Though
> one may be overpowered, two can defend
> themselves. A cord of three strands is not
> quickly broken.

 Word to the Wise

> If you and your fiancé want to write
> separate vows but wish to tie the two
> together, choose one Bible verse, quote,
> or simple statement together that you will
> each recite, followed by your own words
> about what the verse means to you and
> your marriage vows.

Song of Solomon 7:10:

> I belong to my lover, and his desire is for me.

1 John 4:18:

> There is no fear in love. But perfect love drives out fear, because fear has to do with punishment. The one who fears is not made perfect in love.

Song of Solomon 8:6–7:

> Place me like a seal over your heart, like a seal on your arm; for love is as strong as death, its jealousy unyielding as the grave. It burns like blazing fire, like a mighty flame. Many waters cannot quench love; rivers cannot wash it away. If one were to give all the wealth of his house for love, it would be utterly scorned.

Colossians 3:12–14:

> Therefore, as God's chosen people, holy and dearly loved, clothe yourselves with compassion, kindness, humility, gentleness, and patience. Bear with each other and forgive whatever grievances you may have against one another. Forgive as the Lord forgave you. And over all these virtues put on love, which binds them all together in perfect unity.

Proverbs 18:22:

> Whoso findeth a wife findeth a good thing.

Koran 30:21:

> And among His signs is this, that He created
> for you mates from among yourselves, that you
> may dwell in peace and tranquility with them,
> and He has put love and mercy between your
> (hearts): Verily in that are signs for those who
> reflect.

Plenty more passages might inspire you. Here are
a few that work well in wedding ceremonies:

- Ruth 1:16
- John 3:16
- Ephesians 4:25–5:2
- Matthew 7:24–27

Poetry

There's something about reading great poetry
that inspires the poet within us. Read it for inspiration and ideas, or swipe a line or two to quote from
in your wedding vows. Just be sure to give credit
where credit is due; you never know what scholars
will be sitting in the pews listening to the "original" way you've chosen to say "I do."

Here's just a small sampling of the poetry that's
been known to stir passion and fan the flames of
love:

William Shakespeare's "Sonnet 116":

> Let me not to the marriage of true minds
> Admit impediments. Love is not love

Which alters when it alteration finds,
Or bends with the remover to remove:
O no! it is an ever-fixed mark
That looks on tempests and is never shaken;
It is the star to every wandering bark,
Whose worth's unknown, although his height
  be taken.
Love's not Time's fool, though rosy lips and
  cheeks
Within his bending sickle's compass come:
Love alters not with his brief hours and weeks,
But bears it out even to the edge of doom.
If this be error and upon me proved,
I never writ, nor no man ever loved.

William Shakespeare's "Sonnet 18":

Shall I compare thee to a summer's day?
Thou art more lovely and more temperate:
Rough winds do shake the darling buds of May,
And summer's lease hath all too short a date:
Sometime too hot the eye of heaven shines,
And often is his gold complexion dimm'd;
And every fair from fair sometime declines,
By chance, or nature's changing course,
  untrimm'd;
But thy eternal summer shall not fade,
Nor lose possession of that fair thou owest;
Nor shall Death brag thou wander'st in his
  shade,
When in eternal lines to time thou growest;
So long as men can breathe, or eyes can see,
So long lives this, and this gives life to thee.

Elizabeth Barrett Browning's "How Do I Love Thee?":

> How do I love thee? Let me count the ways.
> I love thee to the depth and breadth and height
> My soul can reach, when feeling out of sight
> For the ends of Being and ideal Grace.
> I love thee to the level of every day's
> Most quiet need, by sun and candlelight.
> I love thee freely, as men strive for Right;
> I love thee purely, as they turn from Praise.
> I love with a passion put to use
> In my old griefs, and with my childhood's faith.
> I love thee with a love I seemed to lose
> With my lost saints,—I love thee with the
>   breath,
> Smiles, tears, of all my life!—and, if God
>   choose,
> I shall but love thee better after death.

There are countless poems out there to inspire your romantic side. Get to your nearest library or surf the web to check out these poems and others like them. They'll give you even more reasons to sigh at the beauty and eternity of true love:

- Maya Angelou's "Touched by an Angel"
- William Penn's "Never Marry but for Love"
- Walt Whitman's "Song for the Open Road"
- Roy Croft's "Love"
- Lord Byron's "She Walks in Beauty"
- Elizabeth Barrett Browning's "Sonnets from the Portuguese"

- Pablo Neruda's "Sonnet LXIX"
- James Lawson's "Not from Pride, but from Humility"

Quotations and Other Bits of Wisdom

Sometimes it doesn't take a whole poem to inspire. Sometimes it takes a simple sentence, penned by someone from the eighteenth century, to make you think of love and marriage in a whole new way. Books of quotations are great resources for finding new (old) ways to express timeless sentiments.

One to try is *The International Thesaurus of Quotations.*

> All thoughts, all passions, all delights,
> Whatever stirs this mortal frame,
> All are ministers of Love,
> And feed his sacred flame."
>
> —Samuel Taylor Coleridge, "Love" (1799)

> To love a thing means wanting it to live.
>
> —Confucius Analects (sixth century B.C.E.)

> Unable are the loved to die
> For Love is Immortality.
>
> —Emily Dickinson (circa 1864)

> The love we give away is the only love we keep.
>
> —Elbert Hubbard, *The Note Book* (1927)

Nuptial Nuggets

If you select a quotation or Bible verse to use in your wedding vows, consider attaching that same verse to your wedding favors. That way, the keepsake you give to family and friends will remind them not just of the special day they shared with you, but the beautiful vows you exchanged as well.

The course of true love never did run smooth.
—William Shakespeare, *A Midsummer Night's Dream* (1595–1596)

And when love speaks, the voice of all the gods makes heaven drowsy with the harmony.
—William Shakespeare, *Love's Labor's Lost* (1598)

Where love reigns the impossible may be attained.
—Indian proverb

To me, fair friend, you never can be old
For as you were when first your eye I eyed,
Such seems your beauty still.
—William Shakespeare, "Sonnet CIV" (circa 1600)

It is not in the stars to hold our destiny, but in ourselves.

—William Shakespeare, "Fate"

Life has taught us that love does not consist in gazing at each other but in looking outward together in the same direction.

—Antoine de Saint-Exupery, "The Little Prince" (1943)

Fortune and love befriend the bold.

—Ovid, "Ars Amatoria" (circa 1 B.C.E.)

From *The Prophet*, by Kahlil Gibran:

You were born together, and together you shall be forevermore.
You shall be together when white wings of death scatter your days.
Aye, you shall be together even in the silent memory of God.
But let there be spaces in your togetherness,
And let the winds of the heavens dance between you.
Love one another but make not a bond of love:
Let it rather be a moving sea between the shores of your souls.
Fill each other's cup but drink not from one cup.
Give one another of your bread but eat not from the same loaf.

Sing and dance together and be joyous, but let
each one of you be alone,

Even as the strings of a lute are alone though
they quiver with the same music.

Give your hearts, but not into each other's
keeping.

For only the hand of Life can contain your
hearts.

And stand together, yet not too near together:

For the pillars of the temple stand apart,

And the oak tree and the cypress grow not in
each other's shadow.

Here is an Apache blessing:

Now you will feel no rain, for each of you will
be the shelter for each other. Now you will feel
no cold, for each of you will be the warmth for
the other. Now you are two persons, but there
is only one life before. Go now to your dwell-
ing place to enter into the days of your life
together. And may your days be good and long
upon the earth. Treat yourselves and each
other with respect, and remind yourselves
often of what brought you together. Give the
highest priority to the tenderness, gentleness
and kindness that your connection deserves.
When frustration, difficulty and fear assail your
relationship—as they threaten all relationships
at one time or another—remember to focus on
what is right between you, not only the part
which seems wrong. In this way, you can ride

out the storms when clouds hide the face of the sun in your lives—remembering that even if you lose sight of it for a moment, the sun is still there. And if each of you takes responsibility for the quality of your life together, it will be marked by abundance and delight.

Quotes, Bible passages, and poems can give you more than just inspiration. They can serve as the framework of your wedding vows. This is just what Lyn and Ryan did when they were married in the Unitarian Universalist Church. The couple spent time poring over quotes and passages on love and friendship and then they wrote their entire wedding ceremony together, including their vows:

> *Lyn:* Love is the quality of heart that unites us and all of life and frees us from our separateness.
>
> We vow to love each other not only through ourselves, but through the work around us. To always remind us that we can learn and grow from everyone and everything within our reach. To leave behind our separate, single lives, and fuse ourselves into one.
>
> *Ryan:* The inner light is beyond praise and blame. Like space, it knows no boundaries. We will not be caught up in praising one person or blaming another or in seeking praise or trying to avoid blame ourselves. Such judgments are alien and only serve to trap us in our separateness.

There is a peace that comforts us when we let go and find ourselves wrapped in each other's spirit. Not a promise or a condition, but an epiphany of our love.

Lyn: But love, the first ember to light the heart doesn't go gray and cold when dreams are ruined.

Today we promise to be there when life gets thick. To listen, respond, and understand, just as we would when there isn't a cloud in the sky. We promise to comfort in times of strife and celebrate in times of joy. But also to reach for the light in times of darkness and remember the darkness in times of light.

Ryan: Within you I lose myself, without you, I find myself wanting to be lost again.

We are here today to celebrate the fusion of our lives, the illustration we now paint together. Supporting a vision that breathes life into a third muse. A mutual inseparableness.

Lyn: You don't marry someone you can live with. You marry someone you can't live without.

We will, from this day forward, celebrate our differences and cherish our similarities. And always remember to respect, love, honor, and appreciate each other, ever mindful of how lucky we are to have been trusted with this responsibility of true love.

Lyn and Ryan used their favorite quotes and passages from Unitarian Universalist literature and then expounded on each sentiment to make the vows truly their own.

There is a bit of Shakespeare in all of us, just itching to come out and write the perfect wedding vow. All it takes is a little work and a little creativity—and sometimes a little help from Shakespeare himself.

The Least You Need to Know

- Speak from your heart, and your wedding vows will write themselves.
- Choose your words carefully. The vows you recite on your wedding day will live on in your memories for years to come.
- Find inspiration in literary greats. Some of what's been written before can be perfect for what you want to say now.

Chapter 7

"I Do" ... What?
Articulating Your Feelings

In This Chapter

- Choosing your words carefully
- Avoiding clichés
- Incorporating wedding themes and settings
- Smoothing out your vow and reading it for the public

It's been said that Ernest Hemingway rewrote the final chapter of *Farewell to Arms* 44 times. When asked why he did so much rewriting, his answer was simple: "To get the words right."

If a literary great such as Hemingway struggles, the rest of us should expect to become intimately familiar with the delete button on our keyboards or the eraser on our pencils.

In this chapter, I help you take the rough draft of your wedding vow and polish it into the moving tribute to your partner it was meant to be. And

I give you some tips to make your wedding vow relevant not only to your relationship, but to your wedding day—the season, the setting, a special theme—as well.

A Diamond in the Rough

So you think you've found the right words with which to marry your partner. You've scribbled a heartful of feelings on a piece of paper (or typed them into a computer file), and you're confident they sound pretty good ... but they're not *exactly* right.

First things first: read over the vow you've written, checking to see that you've made the major points you wanted to make. Look back at the notes you took before you started writing, including the questions you answered about your partner and your relationship, and the thoughts you had about what you wanted to hear in the wedding vow given to you.

If you've covered the main points you so painstakingly chose as the most important things to say, then half the battle is won. If you've left out something critical, now's the time to add it—before you begin subtracting things.

"I Choose You ... for a Very Important Reason"

It's said that the difference between a writer and an editor is the ability to see what shouldn't be there. A writer always wants to add more, and an editor always wants to cut things out. Both jobs are important, and when constructing your vow, you're likely serving as both writer and editor.

This is both a burden and a blessing. It's tough to look at your own writing with a critical or even impartial eye. But it's also nice to know that in the editing process, if the writer's own voice and style are stripped in favor of the editor's, it will still sound like you!

The trick to editing is to know that less is usually more. Take, for example, the traditional wedding vow:

> I _____, take you, _____, to be my wedded wife/husband, to have and to hold from this day forward, for better for worse, for richer, for poorer, in sickness and in health, till death do us part.

In less than 40 words, the author has summed up every instance of life for which the couple has pledged to be there for each other: love, support, romance, fidelity, and commitment—all conveyed in that one sentence. Omit any of the words, and you lose some meaning.

Can you say the same of your wedding vow? Take another look at it and see. Read it sentence by sentence, making a note in the margin about what each sentence is conveying. Watch out for redundancies. Are you talking about supporting your future spouse over and over again? If so, consolidate those thoughts into one sentence, or pick the strongest way you've expressed that and omit the others.

Also, look for generic sounding phrases and sentences that, when it comes right down to it, could be about anyone, not just your beloved. Here are a few examples of what I mean:

> My love for you is deeper than the ocean (brighter than the sun, etc.).
>
> Today is the first day of the rest of our lives.
>
> I love you more than words can say.

If it sounds like you've swiped the wording from a cheesy pop song or a sappy greeting card, it's probably a *cliché*.

Language of Love

A **cliché** is an expression or idea that's become trite from overuse. Clichéd phrases have been used so many times they no longer have an ounce of originality. They abound in wedding ceremonies and wedding vows (not to mention wedding toasts), and should be avoided whenever possible.

Most of us have heard some clichés so much that we write them without thinking because they're the first things that pop into our minds. Saying your partner "swept you off your feet" or is "the apple of your eye" will make perfect sense to everyone in attendance because it's been said a million times about a million other brides and grooms.

Therein lies the problem. You're not a million other brides and grooms. You want your vow to be as original as your partner is, so try to eliminate clichés by being as specific to your love story as possible.

Instead of describing your partner as someone who "swept you off your feet," write a sentence that explains the circumstances of the night you met or the day you fell in love. Hearing this will bring your partner back to the magic of that moment, which is really what you're hoping for anyway.

The Weight of Words

With editing comes clarity. You're trying to make each word count, and the ones that don't should be deleted. Don't be abstract. If you've written something too general, change it to something specific. Whenever possible, use bits and pieces of your life together to illustrate your point.

Mike married Sharon just as she was entering medical school. He knew how important her career was to her, and he wanted her to know that he'd be there to help. Mike could have made a broad, sweeping statement such as, "I will support you in all you do," and Sharon would have understood what he meant. But instead, Mike said,

"I promise to give you hot meals after long days of studying and foot massages after long nights at the hospital. While you care for your patients, always I will care for you."

In a few thoughtful examples, Mike conveyed the true nature of his love and devotion for Sharon much better than any generic statement could. Remember, you and your partner are making the effort to write your own wedding vows because you want them to sound personal. Be sure they do!

The flip side to this is writing vows that are so personal your audience can't follow what it is you're trying to say. Also, don't fall into the trap of making sweeping promises to your partner you're not sure you can keep. Vows such as "I will take you on romantic vacations to faraway countries" and "I will spend every holiday with your family because that's what I know you love to do" could come back to haunt you!

Like Mike did for Sharon, stick to giving examples of how you will show your love and devotion in your everyday lives. Chances are, everyone listening will be able to relate. Who wouldn't like a foot rub at the end of a long, hard day?

You can also personalize your vow through the tone you take when writing. The tone can be stuffy, casual, even poetic—but it should sound like *you*.

Nuptial Nuggets

If you're having trouble finding personal anecdotes to add to your vow, take a minute and think of things you already do for your partner (and I don't mean leaving the toilet seat down). Do you wash the dishes when he cooks and vice versa? Do you always give your partner the last bite of dessert? Chances are, your relationship contains a few simple yet important gestures that show your partner you love him. Mentioning even one of them is a great way to recognize a love that you've already made special.

Tone is hard to describe but easy to hear. These statements all say the same thing but in different ways:

> I will fill your arms with love and your life with laughter.

> I pledge to grant you every form of happiness so that our humble abode will always be a sanctuary of love.

> I promise to make ours a happy home.

All three say basically the same thing, but they say it in three distinct voices. That's what tone is all about. The first statement has a poetic cadence, the second is a formal declaration, and the third a simple pledge.

Now look at what you've written. Does it sound like something you would say or write? If not, it's time to revise.

Keep Your Vows Positive

Tone isn't just created by the way you write, but also by the things you say. You don't want your vows to have a negative tone, to be all doom and gloom on such a joyous day. This sounds like a no-brainer, but you'd be surprised by how many brides and grooms include the negative aspects of their collective history in their wedding vows.

True, the valleys in life can bring us even closer together than the peaks, and certainly, if one of you has faced serious hardship or illness, it's natural to want to thank your partner for being there when you needed them most. Here's an example of a vow that serves to thank one's spouse for the past as well as promise her the future:

> Certainly God has brought us here today, to stand together looking into the eyes of someone who reflects the promise—not just the vow to hold hands in this life, but the pledge to help pull and push and coax us up to the next life. You are that person for me, the one who challenges the vices I have come to love, and affirms the gifts I am afraid to claim. The Lord has smiled with every triumph we have shared, wiped away every tear we have shed, gracefully given us every tomorrow we have felt truly blessed to have reached. He has encouraged us

to love one another with arms wide open, as He has always done. This past year, we saw His power reflected in our own eyes, and through it all, that light of faith never dimmed. It is toward that light that this hopeful journey heads, together, hand in hand, ever by faith in each other and by faith in the one who waits for us, his arms wide open.

This vow definitely has a religious tone, one of thankfulness and faith. It hints at something serious that happened in the past year without going into morbid detail. After all, everyone in attendance at that wedding already knew that the groom had spent the better part of a year before battling cancer and was thankful to be in remission and pledging his life to the one who had helped him through it.

The bottom line is to choose wisely about what to include in your vows, and do it in a subtle way. This is not the time to thank your beloved for supporting you through the divorce proceedings from your first marriage or for helping you deal with difficult family members. It's better to speak about the support you have given and will give to each other in general terms. Chances are, your spouse will know exactly what you mean.

Exclude Inside Jokes

This is also not the time, when you're standing up at the altar in front of friends and family, to mention the crazy spring break trip you both took during which you broke up and got back together three times in one week.

Inside jokes and private stories should be kept to yourselves. That's not to say an anecdote or observation about your future spouse should be off limits. But keep in mind that at the end of your vow, you're counting on your partner to actually say "I do." Plus, you might be videotaping the whole thing, so be careful of what tidbits from your life you're exposing for your future children to hear about.

 Word to the Wise

> With each sentence you write, imagine saying that tidbit to your future spouse, your future spouse's mother, and your wedding officiant. If you can't imagine any of those three raising an eyebrow at what you'd like to say, then you're probably safe.

Besides saving yourselves from the embarrassment of publicizing painful or humiliating memories, keeping inside jokes and stories out of your vows keeps your extended audience tuned in to all the positive things you're saying. Your Aunt Renee doesn't know about that spring break trip from long ago, but she does know what you mean when you pledge to be there for your spouse through thick and thin.

When it comes right down to it, writing your wedding vows is like writing a love letter to your partner—one that will be read in front of everyone you know. Piece of cake! It just takes a little thought and a little courage.

Extra Special: Tailoring Your Vows

Many couples select themes around which they plan their big day, incorporating that theme into everything from the party favors to the table centerpieces to the wedding's setting itself.

If you and your partner have chosen a wedding theme that's particularly special to you—a favorite season, a beach setting, a holiday both of you cherish—it might be appropriate to work that theme into your wedding vows.

Themed Weddings

When my sister Kielynn-Marie and her husband, Luis, got married, they knew they wanted a casually elegant affair, and they knew they wanted it at the beach. Both were living in southern California, and the ocean was a big part of their love story.

So when they asked me to write a poem that would be read right after they exchanged wedding vows, I wanted to keep that special theme in mind. I interviewed each of them separately about what they loved most about each other, writing down key words and feelings they described.

I chose to incorporate the waves and the sand and the pull of the tide in my poem, imagining how I would be saying those words with a sunset over the Pacific Ocean as a backdrop. But on the afternoon of the wedding, the wind picked up so much that the nuptials had to be moved inside, behind the safety of a beach house's glassed-in sunroom. Those in attendance watched the waves spill over the deck and mist the glass with sea spray as I read what became an even more relevant bit of prose than what I'd had in mind:

Captured

Drawn in,
like the pull of the moon
sends waves stretching
to drench the sand they crave.
"I was captured,"
he says of her,
unaware that she too
had prayed for such passion,
an equal force
to pull her down
and stand beside her
and lift her to higher ground.
She calls him chivalrous
and optimistic,
attentive and honorable.
And in her eyes he sees
tenderness
and conviction
and support.

How soft yet barren
the sand without the waves.
How strong yet silent
the waves without the sand.
Together, they are magic,
meant to be.
They did not know
how strong they were
until they were mirrored
in each other's soul.
And in that moment
of clarity and beauty
and power
they are undeniable—
soft and strong.
And free.
And home.

The bride, groom, and several of the guests said
they remembered the poem long after the wedding
day because it captured more than a love, it captured the day's entire setting. You can give your
vows that same permanence if you incorporate your
wedding theme when writing them.

But the inclusion can't be contrived; it has to flow
with the sentiments in your vow. If you've chosen
a special theme, you must have a reason. Did you
always want a fall wedding, and if so, why? Is it the
fall foliage you love, the crisp autumn leaves under-
foot? Perhaps your wedding vows can include this
image, alluding to the brilliance and beauty of the
season when talking about the autumn of your
years together.

You can also use poetry that focuses on your wedding's theme. There's no easier way to delve into your vows for a summer-themed wedding than borrowing from Shakespeare's Sonnet 18, "Shall I Compare Thee to a Summer's Day?"

If you'd like to use a theme in your vows, you might want to mention that idea to your partner. Although it's fine for both vows to be as unique as you are, coordinating an overall theme could show the world that as you begin your lives together, you two really are on the same page. (For an example of two vows written using the same theme, see Chapter 5.)

If you want to incorporate your wedding site or theme in your vows, you need to soak up the atmosphere. If you can, go to the ceremony site, spend some time there, and ruminate on what you see, hear, and feel.

Think about why you chose your theme. What does it mean to you and your partner? What does it say about your relationship? When you give yourself a little time to contemplate the choices you've made, chances are the answers can be woven into a very meaningful, memorable wedding vow.

Holiday Nuptials

Holidays can be extra-special times to celebrate your nuptials. The whole world seems festively decorated and especially jubilant at certain times of the year. Some brides and grooms choose to take advantage of all that merrymaking and get married on or around a holiday.

Wedding vows should always center on the loving commitment you're making as husband and wife, but incorporating your holiday theme into the vows themselves can add a memorable touch.

If you're planning a Christmas wedding, chances are you're religious. Such a special day in the life of the Christian Church lends itself to mentioning God's commitment to you and your marriage in your wedding vows.

A New Year's Eve or New Year's Day wedding theme centers around celebrating the old and anticipating the new, and this is exactly what wedding vows should do. Start your vow by focusing on how far you've come, and conclude it with a vision for your future together.

A Thanksgiving wedding is an obvious time to give thanks, both *to* your spouse and *for* your spouse. For Thanksgiving-themed wedding vows, you might mention important people in your partner's life who are in attendance, thanking them for the wisdom and character and guidance they've given your beloved that has led him or her to your side. This would be touching for both your partner and his or her loved ones.

And Valentine's Day weddings ... well, the sky's the limit! Those who marry on Valentine's Day must be hopeless romantics, so be sure your wedding vows reflect such passion and whimsy.

Nuptial Nuggets _____

Holiday weddings are great opportunities for the other couples in attendance to recommit themselves to their marriages or toast to their partners, and you can help everyone else celebrate their love on your special day. If you have a Valentine's Day wedding, let each husband toast his wife. If you tie the knot on New Year's Day, allow each couple to offer a resolution they will commit to for their relationship. And if you have Thanksgiving nuptials, give everyone a chance to stand up and say what or whom they are thankful for.

Putting It All Together

By now your vows probably look quite a bit different from what they looked like in your first draft. But that means you've wielded your editing pen correctly. In *The Word: An Associated Press Guide to Good News Writing*, esteemed Associated Press editor Rene Cappon wrote, "Writing is the art of the second thought."

Before you accept what you've written as your final draft, it's a good idea to run it through a few checks and balances first. You don't want to have a glaring omission in your vow and not realize it until you're standing at the altar giving the most important "speech" of your life.

A Few Final Checks

When reading over your wedding vow one last
time, be sure there's a natural flow, one that your
partner and the rest of those in attendance can
easily follow. You are, in essence, telling a short
story, the story of your love. Your vow should have
a beginning, a middle, and an end. If you've written
about your past, put that near the beginning of
your vow. If you stress your plans for the future,
be sure that's worked in near the end.

 **Word to the Wise** _____

> Your wedding vow is obviously going
> to be a personal statement to your spouse,
> but be sure you say your partner's name at
> least once during your vow. Couples don't
> use each other's names very often, and
> hearing your partner say your name while
> holding your hand and promising forever
> will warm your heart. Trust me.

After you've worked and reworked your wedding
vow, put it away for a while. Don't look at it or
read it for a few hours or a few days. Then come
back to it and read it with fresh eyes and a new
perspective. No doubt it'll sound a bit different
than it did the first hundred times you pored over
it, and that's when you'll catch any awkward statements or miscues.

Read It Aloud

When you think you're done, read your vow out loud. Read slowly and deliberately; don't rush. Pay attention to when you have to pause to take a breath. Your vow needs to be written so you can recite it out loud comfortably and comprehensively, so use punctuation wisely. Hold sentences to the length of one breath. You don't want to be turning blue in the face, rushing to finish your vow before sucking in a giant breath of air.

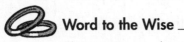 **Word to the Wise**

Chances are you know someone who either writes or speaks publicly for a living. Pass your vow off to such a friend, and have them use their expertise to give you professional advice on how to really make your vow shine.

You also don't want your vow to be too long or too short. Imagine yourself up there at the altar, all eyes on you, while you say these magical words. Have you written what could pass for the chapter of a book? Or is what you say over so quickly people will barely have enough time to comprehend what's happening?

On your wedding day, it's easy for your minds to go blank—it's hard to remember to breathe, let alone comprehend every word said and every promise exchanged. You want your vow to be long enough so your partner has time to focus on your words, but not so long that you begin to stumble over a cumbersome passage.

Review With Officiant

Before you tuck your vow carefully away, review it with your wedding officiant. Sometimes the officiant might have suggestions—or even requirements—to make it an official "vow" according to the rules of the church or synagogue in which you're getting married.

 Word to the Wise

> Let me again emphasize how important it is to check with your officiant beforehand to be sure it's okay for you to write your own wedding vows. You don't want to have worked this hard only to get to your rehearsal and be told you can't use your personal vows after all.

But don't just hand over the words you've written. Sit with your officiant and tell him or her why you chose the words you've written. Explain how you and your partner discussed what was important to both of you in a marriage and in a wedding vow, and how you've tried to incorporate those very important wishes and goals into your vow. The more the officiant hears about how much time, energy, and love went into the writing of your vows, the more apt he or she is to give you the go-ahead.

The Least You Need to Know

- Choose your words carefully to convey the right feelings and tone.
- Let your vows be personal without being too personal. Save inside jokes and anything you wouldn't want your mother to hear for later.
- Use creative ways to incorporate your wedding day theme into your vows.
- Read your wedding vow aloud to be sure it sounds right and is easily readable. Check for the right flow of ideas, from past to present to future.
- Allow your wedding officiant to read and approve your vow prior to your wedding day.

Chapter 8

Special Delivery: Reciting Your Vows

In This Chapter

- Agreeing on a way to exchange vows
- Memorizing your vows?: Tips and tricks
- Practicing for public speaking
- Alternatives to memorizing vows

You've written your wedding vows, so now there's really just one thing left to do: deliver them. To do so, you just have to overcome all manners of stage fright, head-in-the-clouds forgetfulness, and over-whelming emotion. Piece of cake, right?

In this chapter, I help you decide whether you should memorize your vows and, if you decide memorization is the way to go, give you some tips on how to do it. I also review some alternate ways to deliver your vows that take less memorization skills but pack just as much of an emotional punch.

To Memorize or Not to Memorize?

Reciting the wedding vows you've carefully written and memorized can make for the most touching moment in your ceremony. When you've truly taken ownership of those words, when they fall from your lips like a song you know by heart, your partner and everyone in attendance will know how much your vow means to you.

Nuptial Nuggets

Even if you haven't written your own wedding vows, you can personalize this part of your ceremony by memorizing the traditional vows you've chosen to use. Ask your officiant if each of you can recite the vow in its entirety from memory instead of repeating it in sections, prompted by the officiant, as it's usually done.

Conversely, trying to recite vows you've attempted to memorize without much success can be painful to watch. The audience and even your fiancé will be distracted, no longer paying attention to what you're saying, only to how poorly you're saying it. I have been to weddings where I just wished for it to be over, wanting to put the hapless bride and groom out of their misery. This is obviously what you want to avoid.

You can memorize your vows and recite them poetically if you first recognize the various pitfalls related to memorizing your vows. It also helps to acknowledge whether you're the type of person who will feel comfortable up there in the spotlight, reciting from memory a list of very important personal statements. Not everyone is cut out for such added pressure on what is already the biggest day of his or her life.

All Heads on Cloud Nine

Getting married is something like giving birth, in that when it's all said and done, you're left with this warm, loving glow and a mountain of happiness, yet you often have only a vague recollection of what was said and done during the actual event.

If I've heard it once, I've heard it a hundred times by a hundred brides and grooms: "I don't even remember what was said while I was up there."

I'm convinced the real reason people videotape their weddings is so they'll be able to go back and watch what actually happened to fill in their memory gaps. Sure, they may say it's so they can one day show their children what happened on the day their parents got married. But in reality, I think the most astute brides and grooms know they probably won't remember much about their own nuptials, so they're gonna need proof of what they actually said.

"No, not me," you might say. "I'll remember every word, every prayer, every tear of joy that trickles down my beloved's cheeks." I hope that's true, but I'm here to prepare you for the reality of most weddings. You'll have so many thoughts and emotions running through your mind—seeing the many details you've planned come to fruition, noticing people in the crowd, noting the way the flowers look at the altar—that you'll likely suffer from serious sensory overload.

 Word to the Wise

> Many brides and grooms who go through the painstaking process of writing their own vows want to keep them a secret until the moment they're delivering them at the altar. But to avoid the emotional overload and the tongue-tied forgetfulness so common in that moment, why not share your vows with each other prior to the big day?
>
> It will give you and your partner the chance to fully digest and appreciate the promises you're about to make.

So when you're thinking about adding the extra stress of reciting memorized wedding vows, consider that when the time comes to say "I do," even those people with the very best concentration skills can find themselves caught up in the moment, their minds blank.

Bashful Brides and Modest Men

It's been said that the number-one fear among Americans is public speaking. The number-two fear is death. As comedian Jerry Seinfeld said, "That means that if you're at a funeral, most people would rather be in the casket than delivering the eulogy."

That should tell you something about how much most of us dread standing in front of a crowd of people—even friends and family—delivering any sort of speech.

When Pamela and James got married, Pam coerced James into delivering their wedding vows without the help of their pastor. Pam reasoned that because they chose to use a slightly altered version of the traditional Christian wedding vows, both of them practically already knew the vow by heart anyway, having heard "for richer, for poorer, in sickness and in health" a million times on television, in movies, and at other weddings.

But what Pam failed to consider was the depth of James's insecurities about public speaking. He already had asked the pastor to keep the ceremony as short as possible because he was so uncomfortable standing up in front of the 100 people they'd invited.

James did his best to keep his nervous anxiety a secret from Pam—until the night before the wedding. That's when it all came spilling out—he was "dreading" the ceremony because of the vows.

This left Pam feeling hurt and anxious, realizing that what seemed like no big deal to her had in fact been a source of great apprehension to her soon-to-be husband.

Although it's true that opposites attract—we've all seen the bookworm with the athlete, the class clown with the shy gal—when it comes to delivering your wedding vows, you both need to be on the same page.

Nuptial Nuggets

If you've agreed to recite your vows from memory but are having trouble getting over your apprehension about public speaking, consider that once you're holding your fiancé's hand, it's likely the rest of the world will dissolve away. That's one magical thing about weddings, so try not to worry. When that moment comes, chances are you'll feel like you're the only two people in the world.

If one of you is painfully shy, the thought of having to memorize and deliver such personal feelings and promises can make even the most love-stricken bride or groom break out into a cold sweat.

You'll have enough minor things to stress over on your wedding day (not that you should). Don't add to the pressure by forcing your shy partner to do something he or she really isn't comfortable doing.

If you're bashful but want to grant your partner's wedding day wish to recite your vows from memory, take heart. According to famed public speaking guru Dale Carnegie, there are three keys to successful public speaking: The speaker must know the topic well, care about the topic, and really want to share the topic with the audience. You've got these three sewn up!

You know your love for and devotion to your partner better than anyone. You care for her passionately. And you're getting married just so you can tell her, and everyone else you know, just that! Looks like you've already got what it takes to "wow" the crowd with your wedding vows. Try to relax and realize that, if this were a class, you'd get an A without breaking a sweat.

Memorization Tricks of the Trade

If you're both set on memorizing your vows, you have a few ways to do it. Everyone retains information in different ways. Some are visual learners, geared toward retaining information when it's translated into images for the mind to conjure up. Others are auditory learners, remembering things from sheer repetition of words and sounds.

No matter how you retain information, a few memorization tips can help your exchange of vows be a flawlessly sentimental highlight of the day.

Start Early

If you're brave enough to want to recite your vows from memory, it's essential that you start memorizing them long before the big day.

Carl and Beth thought writing their own wedding vows was the most romantic gesture they'd ever heard of. They conferred with their officiant early on and got the green light to compose their own.

But then the wedding planning got busy, with DJs to interview, caterers to meet, and a million other details to work out. As the day approached, Carl and Beth considered scrapping their original plan and going with traditional vows. But the dream of having original vows was too strong.

Nuptial Nuggets

If you've taken the time to write your own vows, get more mileage out of them by having them framed as a wedding gift for your partner. You can enlist the help of a calligrapher or just have them printed on high-quality paper. Be sure to include your names and wedding date. Then have them matted and framed for a heartfelt keepsake of your special day.

Carl managed to write his, mostly during down time at the office, but Beth was so swamped with last-minute wedding details that she was still composing and memorizing hers the night before the wedding!

When it came time to deliver the vows, Carl did okay but Beth was stumped. After stammering through her first sentence, she gave up trying to recite what she'd written and ended up just speaking from her heart. Beth's words were as touching as Carl's, but she still wishes she'd made memorizing the vows more of a priority.

As your wedding day approaches, your mind will be buzzing with dress fittings, seating charts, and honeymoon dreams. So before your brain is clogged with last-minute details, find time to get your vows stored up there, too.

Break It Down

You've probably spent a good deal of time thinking about, writing, and editing your vow, so even if you think it'll be impossible to remember what you've written, chances are half of it is already tucked safely away in the far recesses of your mind. The trick is memorizing the rest of it and being able to recall it during one of the most stressful moments of your life.

Here are a few helpful hints for committing your wedding vow to memory:

- Work on two sentences at a time. This will make it easier to string together the entire vow.

- When you're memorizing the vow, say it aloud. Hearing the vow over and over helps you memorize it faster and helps you recall it better than if you memorize it silently.

- Give each sentence a one-word summary, and memorize those words. Thinking about each of those words should jog your memory on each sentence in your vow.

- If you're a visual person, try to think of an image to associate with each sentence or thought. This technique, known as *loci*, enables you to create a mental scrapbook of your vow. Remembering those images should make it easier to remember what sentiment or promise is attached to each imaginary snapshot.

Language of Love

The **loci** memory technique involves thinking of a familiar building or path—your own house, for example, or the drive you take from your home to the store. Pick specific landmarks you see along the way as you mentally walk that path (the front door, the couch, the television) and then associate a thought or sentiment you're trying to memorize with each landmark.

No matter what tricks you use to help memorize your vow, the bottom line is to practice, practice, practice. Recite your vow in the shower. Say it while looking at a photograph of your fiancé.

Practice in front of the mirror. Or ask a trusted friend or sibling to stand and listen as you promise your life and love to them. (Then laugh as they say "I don't.")

Short-Term Memory? Some Alternatives

Some people will only feel confident once they know their wedding vows word for word. But keep in mind that delivering a memorized speech word for word can end up sounding a little stilted, a bit too rehearsed. You want the emotion of the day to be conveyed in your words.

 Word to the Wise _____

> It's essential to practice looking someone in the eye when delivering your vow. You don't want to look like you did in seventh grade when you had to memorize Lewis Carroll's "Jabberwocky" and you squinted and closed your eyes and looked off into space as you recited the poem aloud. Find a willing friend, and practice delivering your vow to a live person, looking them in the eye.

This is not to say you shouldn't spend considerable, thoughtful time practicing. Just be sure to memorize the main points, including key words and phrases, so that on the big day you can speak from your heart but not forget what you wanted to say.

Memorizing your vows can also be a good way to really know whether you've written them clearly. Is there any tricky wording or phrasing your tongue and memory keep tripping on? Does the vow seem to jump around from your future to your past to your present and back to your past?

Don't be afraid to go back and rework your words a little bit. Chances are your mind knows what it wants to say. If you keep messing up and saying something that is just a bit different from what's on the page, listen to your brain. That's probably the way you should say it anyway.

Go With the Flow

Sometimes even when you keep your head together enough to remember your lines, your best intentions can get derailed by unforeseen wedding day mishaps.

Jean and Ed chose to exchange the traditional Christian vows suggested by their minister. But when the moment came, Jean says, something went terribly awry.

"When Ed was supposed to say his vow to me, the sun was in his eyes and he couldn't see me," Jean says. "So the minister asked us to move closer, but Ed sees double vision when I get too close, so I looked like a Cyclops to him. We had to stop because he was getting dizzy looking at me."

Good-natured brides and grooms can look back on such mishaps with laughter, but the point is that your wedding day can cause all sorts of minor stresses. So whether you choose to memorize your lines or not, be prepared for unexpected things that can make you lose your train of thought.

Confer With the Officiant

Your wedding officiant has no doubt seen and heard it all. They are professionals who can be trusted to help you pull off the wedding you always wanted, glitches and all. Talk to your officiant not only about what your vows entail but how you will exchange them. Experienced wedding officiants know what works best and what doesn't, so use their knowledge to help you.

The officiant will take into consideration things you may not have thought about. Are you getting married on the beach? You may need to use a microphone so your vows can be heard over the crashing waves on the shore.

Your officiant also will take a look at the length of your vows and can tell you if they're running a bit long or seem too short for the kind of ceremony you are planning.

Cheat Sheet

No matter how much memorizing one does, there's no such thing as being overprepared when it comes to delivering your wedding vows. So even if you think you've got it all down pat, don't be afraid to take some precautionary measures to ensure your success.

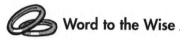

Word to the Wise

> If you don't want to share your vows with each other before your wedding day, it's still a good idea to share them with your wedding officiant. The officiant can tell you, without disclosing what each of you wrote, whether they're very different in the promises being made or sentiments expressed.
>
> Remember, even though you want both vows to be original and heartfelt, you want to be on the same page. Let a trusted third party be sure you are.

Weddings are solemn and sentimental, but nobody's grading you. You can use cheat sheets! On an index card, jot down the major points, key words, or phrases in your wedding vow that will jog your memory if need be.

Grooms can stick this cheat sheet in their pocket, and brides can discreetly wrap it around their flowers or have one of their bridesmaids hold it until it's needed.

Another good idea is for both of you to give a copy of your vows to the officiant. That way she can steer you in the right direction if you wander off course.

Call and Answer

Many brides and grooms use the tried-and-true "call-and-answer" method to exchange their vows.

The officiant can help you recite them to each other line by line by repeating what he says.

As an alternative, have the officiant recite one phrase or sentence and then after you repeat that line, elaborate using the personalized vow you've written. For example, have the officiant start by saying ...

> I, _____, promise to love you, _____ with all that I am and all that I have.

Then you repeat this line, adding a few sentences of your own to better explain how you will do this ...

> I, Daniel, promise to love you, Maria, with all that I am and all that I have. My every possession, my every dream is yours to share. Today I am a far better person than when I met you, for you have given me the courage to be the kind of person who makes you proud. All that I am is a product of your love and a hope for our tomorrows. I humbly give it all to you.

This method ensures that both vows make similar promises, but it allows for the individuality that comes with including your own thoughts and feelings as well.

Yet another alternative is to have the officiant whisper the vows, one sentence at a time, to you and have you repeat them aloud to your beloved. The priest who married Steven and Wendy did just that. Wendy says they hadn't intended to memorize their vows, but because of the priest's whispering trick, the wedding guests believed the couple had done just that. Family and friends came up to her after the nuptials to say how touching it was to see the bride and groom recite their vows from memory, and she was very grateful for the priest's cleverness!

Best of Both Worlds

If you'd like to say a few words about your spouse but don't want the pressure of those words being your formal vow, ask the officiant if you can both take a few moments to speak to each other candidly before exchanging traditional vows.

That way you can say what you want to say, knowing that your solemn vows of marriage aren't hinging on whether or not you flub your lines.

The Least You Need to Know

- Be sure both you and your fiancé are okay with reciting your vows from memory.
- Begin memorizing your vows several weeks before the ceremony.
- Use memorization tricks to get your wedding vows down pat.

- Confer with your officiant about how you would like to exchange your vows.

- Think about using a crutch, such as a cheat sheet, to boost your confidence about reciting your vow.

- Consider an alternative to reciting your vows entirely from memory.

Chapter 9

The Second Time Around

In This Chapter

- Deciding when to renew your vows
- Writing vows about your marriage
- Writing vows for second weddings
- Including your children in your vows

Saying wedding vows for the second time can mean several things. For spouses who have been married for many years, renewing vows can be even more romantic than the first time around. In saying "I do" all over again, you are saying you cherish everything the two of you have shared by recommitting your life to each other. That's a beautiful thing.

If you've been married before, exchanging wedding vows with someone new is an important expression of what they mean to you and what a beautiful life the two of you are promising to share.

In this chapter, I discuss the myriad ways couples can choose to renew their vows. And I help second-time brides and grooms find just the right words with which to pledge their eternal love to a brand-new spouse. I also offer tips on how and when to include children and other family members in your wedding vows.

"I Do ... Again": Vow Renewals

Amy and BJ got married in their early 20s. Their love was strong, but it was a stressful time, with Amy trying to finish her degree and BJ working hard to support them. As the years flew by, their marriage grew stronger and stronger. Theirs was a great love story, but they always looked back on their wedding day with mixed emotions, remembering the stress they'd felt at the time.

They thought about renewing their vows on their tenth anniversary but ultimately decided not to wait. They booked a romantic weeklong vacation getaway at a posh couples-only resort in the Bahamas for their eighth anniversary, found a local wedding officiant, and renewed their vows on the beach. Both say it was the best thing they could have done for their marriage.

Renewing your wedding vows, after 3 years or 30, brings you back to the beginning, back to the basics of why you're together and what you're supposed to be providing each other with in this life.

Many couples who got married years ago used traditional wedding vows because writing their own was unheard of or forbidden in their place of worship. But times and trends have changed. Writing original vows for a vow renewal ceremony gives you a chance to express the depth of emotion you've come to know and cherish in the time you've spent as husband and wife.

Plus, if yours has been like most marriages, you've no doubt been down many roads together, good and bad, that have enriched your lives and your love. In other words, you've got a lot to say!

When to Renew Vows

Often people think of a vow renewal ceremony as something that's done on a big anniversary— 10, 25, even 50 years. But as with most gestures of love, there's no need to wait for a monumental occasion. Do it when both of you feel it would benefit your relationship.

Bob and Sue were happily married for 12 years with 2 beautiful children when Sue was diagnosed with breast cancer. After spending the next 3 years battling the disease, with relapse after relapse, the cancer finally went into remission for good and the family was able to get on with their lives.

Bob and Sue had always planned to renew their wedding vows on their twentieth anniversary. But Sue's brush with cancer and the way it affected their family made them realize there was no time like the present to gather loved ones together and say to each other "I *still* do."

Filled with gratitude and love for what they'd both been through, their vow renewal ceremony packed an extra emotional punch. And the occasion was made even more joyous by Sue's ever-improving health.

There is no "correct" time to renew wedding vows. You have to decide when the prefect time is for you and your relationship. Have you both been through some monumental changes or hardships in recent years like Bob and Sue? When you see the light at the end of that tunnel, it's a great idea to stand and thank the one who held your hand through the darkness.

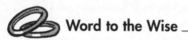

Word to the Wise

Remember that a vow renewal ceremony should be a romantic decision the two of you make together. And it should be a relatively stress-free occasion. This is not the time to plan another full-scale wedding and reception (unless you didn't have one the first time around). Keep it simple and focused on recommitting yourselves to each other.

Have you both been so blessed with happiness and good fortune that you'd like to take an opportunity to thank each other, God, and your loved ones for the support you've been given? A vow renewal ceremony can be a way to acknowledge those you love while you look even more hopefully into the future.

Has the rush of life and everyday stresses shifted the focus of your marriage a little off track? Renewing your wedding vows can be just the romantic spark you've been hoping for to rekindle the passion and recapture the romance in your relationship.

Tried and True: Reciting Your Original Vows

If you've decided to hold a vow renewal ceremony, the first decision you should make is about what you'll say. Chances are, if enough time has gone by between now and when you last said "I do," you probably don't remember word for word what you said the first time. Even the traditional wedding vows have several variations.

It's a lot of fun to dig out your old wedding video and watch yourselves exchange those solemn vows. If you don't have a wedding video, try to track down your wedding officiant or the church where you got married and ask what the standard wedding vow was at that time.

There's something hopelessly romantic about looking into each other's eyes and reciting the original vows you exchanged years ago. Plus, those traditional wedding vows that have been said by thousands of couples for decades are timeless. They're as relevant to your first day of marriage as they are to your 7,300th day of marriage.

Nuptial Nuggets

If you want to exchange your original vows but update them, think about the way you said them the first time. If you didn't recite the vows from memory, try that this time. Or take your original vow and add to it, including some thoughts about what you have done and will do to make those promises come true.

In with the New: Writing New Vows

As classic as your original wedding vows were, sometimes there's just more to say at a vow renewal ceremony. You've had ups and downs, good fortune and sudden crises. You've moved, struggled, raised a family, and supported each other's careers. You want to let your partner know how much all that has meant to you.

When it comes to writing vows for a vow renewal ceremony, the trick is not to get overwhelmed. At this point in your lives, you could probably write chapters on your love story. But what you're aiming for with this new vow is a synopsis of how far you've come, how you feel about the person today, and what your hopes are for the future.

Sounds simple, right? Not quite.

When writing for vow renewals it's important to take time first to reflect on your relationship and on the person you married.

Think about your years together. Ask yourself—or each other—these questions, and jot down your thoughts:

- What successes and failures have you had that brought you closer?
- How did you weather those sunny days and stormy times together?
- How did your spouse rise to the most difficult challenges in your marriage?
- Think about what your partner was like the day you got married compared with who that person is today. How has your partner changed? What about his or her character is exactly the same?
- Think about holidays and other special times. What traditions have you started and cherish as a family?
- What have been the happiest moments in your marriage? What made them so joyous?
- What dreams and plans do you have for the future?

Once you spend some time pondering your history together, you'll be able to touch on the highlights of your marriage and express the feelings you have for the one who's been by your side through it all. Try to be specific, without retelling every tale the two of you have shared. (Save those for a humorous, heartfelt toast later in the day.)

Nuptial Nuggets _____

If you're planning to renew your vows on a particular anniversary date, consider using that year's anniversary theme as a central symbol in your wedding vows. A symbolic gift that coincides with each anniversary year, including ...

1 year: paper	*20 years:* china
5 years: wood	*25 years:* silver
10 years: tin, aluminum	*30 years:* pearl
15 years: crystal	*50 years:* gold

Clarissa and David, married for 25 years, were inspired to renew their wedding vows after witnessing their daughter's nuptials. Watching her happiness brought them right back to their own wedding day, and they wanted to celebrate that love publicly again, this time allowing their children to share in their joy.

Clarissa's vow to David shows the depth of her love for him:

David, it's amazing to me that a quarter-century has gone by and I still get to hold your hand. I knew I was marrying the man of my dreams, but back then I didn't really know what that meant. What I have learned is that the man of my dreams is someone who will nudge me when I am afraid and support me when I fall, without ever letting me feel like a failure. My dream man is someone who gives me two beautiful children and then makes our home the kind of place where James and Karen and all their friends want to be.

My perfect mate is someone who can take an overnight camping trip and turn it into a cherished family tradition.

My dream man is someone who sees me when I'm sick and when I'm grumpy, he sees me as a mother and a grandmother, and he still makes me feel like the most beautiful woman in the world.

I look into your eyes all these years later, and I see the man I married—the man of my dreams. I loved you yesterday, I love you today, and I will love you all the days of my life.

David's vow to Clarissa was just as touching:

Clarissa, 25 years have gone by in a flash but have left us with a lifetime of memories. You have guided this marriage down a path that's been far more fulfilling than I could have ever imagined.

When I look at James and Karen, I see your smile and your devotion, and I am over-whelmed with gratitude and love for the family you have blessed us with.

I love you for your angelic spirit, your Christmas cookies, and your ability to turn one soggy camping trip into a lasting tradition. I love you for your selflessness; for your big, beautiful brown eyes; for the way you worry too much; and most of all for the way you've lit up every room you've ever entered, from that first day we met until today.

I loved you yesterday, I love you today, and I will love you all the days of my life.

Clarissa and David chose to end their vows with the same simple statement to symbolize that they still are on the same page as they look forward to another 25 years together.

 Nuptial Nuggets

Did you plan to exchange personalized vows but then get cold feet? Even if you and your spouse are opting to scrap your original vows and use the traditional vows instead, don't throw out any notes you took about your beloved. You probably have a good start on the perfect wedding day toast to your longtime love, or a love letter to give them the morning of your big day. Such sweet sentiments should never go to waste!

Other vows for recommitment ceremonies talk more about the future than the past:

> It's been 20 years, but every day is brand new, and I stand here today vowing my life to you as if for the very first time. I will do my best to live every day in such a way that you feel as honored to stand by my side as I have always felt to stand beside you. I will comfort you and cherish you, nurture your strengths and ease your fears, for as long as we both shall live. Whatever this world has in store for us, let us hold hands and rejoice in knowing our souls have found their perfect mates.

And this vow speaks to the fresh start the vow renewal ceremony may grant to the marriage:

> The day I married you, the mere word *marriage* was one of those beautiful, frightening unknowns that made my heart flutter with anticipation of what could be and what would be. And now here I stand beside you again, all these years later, eager and thankful for that same flutter in my heart as we take a new step, a bold step, a familiar step in a beautiful new direction. All our yesterdays, both the good and the bad, have brought us to this moment—to my hand in yours, my heart in your hands, and my dream for our love.

Once Again, with Feeling: Vows for Second Marriages

Sometimes, love blooms more than once in a lifetime. And when it does, it is an occasion to celebrate!

At one time, it was taboo to celebrate second marriages with anything more than a simple ceremony for close friends and family. The bride shouldn't wear white, the father of the bride shouldn't give his daughter away … there were tons of etiquette rules about how to say "I do" if you'd already said it before.

But times have changed. Today couples getting remarried are opting to have more elaborate, traditional wedding ceremonies and receptions. A traditional ceremony can become intensely personal and unique to your new union with the exchanging of your own original wedding vows.

For someone getting remarried, writing your vows is a great way to tell your fiancé—and the rest of the world—just how much he or she means to you. But there are some pitfalls to avoid.

Leave the Baggage Behind

If you're getting remarried, the most important thing to keep in mind when writing your wedding vows is to focus on your partner. Speak to your beloved about the present and the future. Mention the past only as it's relevant to your love story.

Nobody, not even your beloved, wants to hear about how thankful you are he or she supported you through the end of your last marriage.

Nuptial Nuggets _____

If you're planning a second wedding and are feeling like you're the only bride in the world who's wary about wearing white, take heart: more than 40 percent of weddings today involve at least one person who is getting remarried. Chances are several of the married couples in attendance at your nuptials have walked in your shoes and will view your vow exchange with knowing smiles, remembering how magical it is when you find a perfect match. They won't care what color your dress is, and you shouldn't either.

Wedding vows are not appropriate venues for you to dredge up the past in a deeply personal way. If you feel the need to say something about how far you've come, say just that. Keep it general; your spouse will still know what you're referring to.

Instead, concentrate on the maturity and wisdom you both bring to the union and the future you look forward to together.

This vow, perfect for second weddings, focuses on marriage as a partnership:

> I, _____, take you _____ to be my wife/husband, my partner in life, and my one true love. I will cherish our friendship and love you today, tomorrow, and forever. I will trust you and honor you. I will laugh with you and cry with you. I will love you faithfully. What may come I will always be there. As I have given you my hand to hold, so I give you my life to keep.

And this one centers on gratitude for one's spouse:

> _____, you are the light that fills my life. I wake up in the morning eager to discover what another day with you will bring, and that is such an awesome feeling. I have hope and joy, gratefulness and compassion, all because of you. In you, I have found someone who will shoulder my burdens and delight in my successes. I know I have found my soul mate and friend. By your side is where I feel at home. I vow to be true to you, to care for, love, and respect you, from this day forward, till death do us part.

And this vow simply speaks to the hopeless romantic in us all:

> I don't ever want to wake up, if it's all dreams. My eyes are wide with wonder at how your

smile makes my heart wish I could see your smile eternally, how your hands call to mine to hold, how you keep me close to you. When all my heroes have fallen, there will be one heart always that can comfort me. And when all your heroes fall, I will be there to remind you that they live inside of you. And when these bodies finally fall, and our heroes can no longer live in them, our souls will forever remember those days and this love as eternity smiles upon us. But my eyes will always remain wide open with wonder of how perfect and whole you've made me. And my soul will sing louder than the angels.

 **Word to the Wise**

> When planning your nuptials, be mindful to select wedding vows, songs, and readings that were not said, read, or sung at your previous wedding. This wedding is a fresh start to a new life with your partner, so let the ceremony stand as a true original as well.

Family Focus

Often when two people marry for the second time, they're blending families as well as hearts. When you have children in the picture, it's essential that they be made to feel like they are an important part of the wedding and the marriage.

Younger children can serve as flower girls or ring bearers, and older children can be junior bridesmaids or contribute by reading a Bible passage or poem. Some brides even choose to have their children walk them down the aisle.

Nuptial Nuggets

Lighting the unity candle takes on an extra-special meaning when you can involve your children. Allowing your children to light the candle using their own separate flames lets them see that they are an active part of the creation of this new union.

Also consider your children when selecting your wedding vows. Some couples like to include their children in the vows they exchange with each other, realizing that the children's upbringing will be a central part of their new life together:

> I Donna, take you, Mark, to be my husband. I promise to love and honor you all the days of my life with all that I have and all that I am. I enter this marriage with my eyes and my heart wide open, anxious to share your dreams and ease your fears. I will strive to be not only a loving wife but a close and trusted friend and guardian to Ben, whom I love and cherish as my own child. You are the two most important

men in my life, and I will love you both, always.

Here's another way to work the children in your vows:

> Christine, I never thought I would find a woman like you. When I first saw you, I thought you were beautiful. But then I saw you with your children, Emily and Chris, and your beauty increased tenfold. I was searching for the mother of my future children, not knowing that my perfect family was already out there. I will do everything in my power to see that your needs, and the needs of Emily and Chris, are always met.

Sam and Rita chose to center their vows on their promises of support and fidelity to each other. But then they offered a special vow to their children:

> Lily and Tommy, we promise to be faithful to your needs, to support and care for you in good times and in bad, in sickness and in health. We will love you and laugh with you, play with you, and pray for you. We know that a happy family is one that knows how to compromise, and we will do that. But we will never compromise our love for you.

> **Word to the Wise**
>
> If your children are old enough, con-
> sider asking them to write their own vow
> to give to you and your partner during the
> ceremony. This allows them to express
> their feelings for their parents, both old
> and new, and explain how they will take
> a positive, active role in their new family.

Including your children in your nuptials will start
your family off on the right foot. When Laura got
married, she not only was becoming a wife to Jack,
but was also stepping into the role of mother to
Jack's 7-year-old daughter, Shelly. Though Laura
and Shelly had hit it off from the start, the little
girl was still close to her biological mother and was
unsure of how happy she should be about her dad's
new bride.

Laura felt it was important to let Shelly know that
they could have a special relationship without
Shelly having to give up any bonds she had with
her parents. So on her wedding day, after exchanging vows with Jack, Laura asked Shelly to come
forward and she presented the little girl with a
heart-shape locket.

Laura vowed to love and cherish the girl as her
own daughter, to be her friend and confidant.
Then she told her to open the locket; inside was a
picture of Shelly's mother. Laura told Shelly that
when she opened the locket and saw her mother's

face she would be reminded of the special bond that only a mother and daughter can share, but that when she wore the locket, she hoped Shelly would think of Laura, who also loved her very, very much.

That simple gesture gave Shelly permission to love and accept both women in her life and to be truly happy for her father.

Practice Makes Perfect

When it comes to writing vows for second marriages, you've got time on your side. That is to say you're likely a more mature person because of the path you've walked thus far in your life. You know what you want, and you know how rare true love is. Use your maturity and honesty to craft the kind of wedding vows that speak of your love for your partner.

All it takes is some careful consideration and honesty (and perhaps a little editing), and I guarantee you can come up with the perfect words to express how you feel, the kind of words that make women swoon and grown men cry, the kind of words that will be met with an enthusiastic "I do!" Good luck!

The Least You Need to Know

- A vow renewal ceremony allows you and your partner to recommit yourselves to your marriage.
- When crafting marriage renewal vows, tell your own love story.

- Use original wedding vows for a second marriage to celebrate the uniqueness of your union.

- Consider ways to include your children in your wedding vows.

- Lean on your own life experiences and wisdom to know the right kind of vows to exchange for second marriages.

Glossary

adjective   A part of speech that modifies a noun.

adverb   A part of speech that modifies a verb, adjective, or other adverb. Usually ends in -ly.

bedeken   The veiling of the bride ritual in Jewish wedding ceremony. Symbolizes the level of modesty a new bride should have.

bridal capture   An ancient tradition whereby the groom literally kidnapped his bride from her family's home.

bride-price   The money and property given to a prospective bride's family by the groom and his family.

Buddhism   An Eastern religion and philosophy that teaches that right thinking and self-denial will enable the soul to reach Nirvana, a divine state of release from misdirected desire.

catholic   Universal or whole. The Catholic faith includes those in the universal Christian Church headed by the pope, such as the Roman, Greek Orthodox, or Anglo-Catholic denominations.

Christian A person who believes in Christianity, the monotheistic religion that recognizes Jesus as the messiah and follows his teachings.

chuppah (pronounced *hup-pah*) A cloth canopy under which a Jewish couple ties the knot. In ancient times, Jewish weddings took place in the groom's tent. Today's symbolic use of the chuppah is meant to signify the couple's new home.

cliché An expression or idea that's become trite from overuse.

Declaration of Intent An element of traditional Christian wedding ceremony that asks bride and groom their intentions for marriage, to which they respond "I do."

dowry The property (land, cash, or goods) a woman brings to her husband for marriage.

handfasting A betrothal signaled by the joining of hands. Different cultures express this tradition in different ways, including tying the bride and groom's wrists or articles of clothing together.

Hindu A person born or living in India or on the Indian subcontinent, or a follower of Hinduism, an ancient religious tradition of India. Hinduism follows the doctrines of karma (the cumulative effects of a person's actions), dharma (universal law), and samsara (the cycle of rebirth).

Islam The monotheistic religion of Muslims. The supreme deity is Allah, and the chief prophet and founder is Muhammad. The basics of the religion are detailed in the holy book the Koran.

Judaism   A monotheistic religion based on the teachings of the Old Testament, the Torah, and the Talmud. Members of a cultural community whose religion is Judaism are called Jews.

ketubah   (plural *ketubot*) The Jewish marriage contract, traditionally written in Aramaic, the language of the Talmud, and signed by two male witnesses.

kiddushin   (also *erusin*) The Jewish betrothal ceremony, formalizing the taking of the bride by the groom. Traditionally includes a gift of a ring from the groom to his bride.

loci   A memory technique that involves thinking of a familiar building or path, selecting specific landmarks along the way as you mentally walk that path and associating a thought or sentence you're trying to memorize with each landmark.

metaphor   A figure of speech in which a word is applied to an object or action as a symbol, not as its true meaning.

nissuin   The Jewish marriage ceremony. Centers on seven blessings for the bride and groom, celebrating their union and thanking God for creating it.

noun   A part of speech that identifies a person, place, or thing.

Orthodox   Strictly adhering to the most traditional laws of Judaism.

Pre-cana   Premarital counseling classes required in the Catholic Church.

saptapadi   Seven Steps taken in a Hindu wedding ceremony, during which the bride and groom recite seven blessings for their marriage.

secular   Describes activities or attitudes that have no religious or spiritual attachment.

simile   A figure of speech used to compare two things using *like* as part of the comparison.

solemn   A sacred in character, serious, or grave; deeply earnest.

tone   In writing, the quality of the words used that reveals the author's voice.

troth   Faithfulness, loyalty, truth.

unity candle   A ceremony that became popular in the 1990s in which the bride and groom light two individual taper candles and then use those tapers to light one larger candle, a symbol of their two lives becoming one.

verb   A part of speech that denotes action.

Resources

The books and websites listed in this appendix provide more information about wedding vows, religious traditions, and other details of the wedding planning process. Have fun!

Websites

These websites put wedding planning at your fingertips, providing help with everything from ceremony reading selection to state-by-state marriage laws.

Art Ketubah
www.artketubah.com
An art source for the Jewish wedding. Order a personalized ketubah online, or sign up for a free catalog.

Beliefnet
beliefnet.com
A spiritual education and information guide. Has articles pertaining to just about anything related to religion and spirituality.

Bible.org
www.bible.org
A biblical reference guide with wedding ceremony samples.

Brilliant Wedding Pages
www.bwedd.com
A personalized wedding website service. Couples can keep guests updated on all the wedding plans. Includes a section of sample wedding vows.

IslamiCity.com
www.islamicity.com
An Islamic educational resource. Learn about Islam, search the Koran for specific verses, share thoughts and ideas about marriage and weddings on the Islamicity.com message boards.

Judaism 101
www.jewfaq.org
An online encyclopedia of Judaism. Includes a fairly thorough section on the Jewish wedding and marriage in Judaism.

Marriage License Laws and Wedding Requirements
straylight.law.cornell.edu/topics/Table_ Marriage.htm
Gives state-by-state marriage laws, including age of consent to marry, whether any type of medical exam is necessary, and how long the marriage license is valid.

MyJewishLearning.com
www.myjewishlearning.com
An online Jewish resource that breaks down the
Jewish wedding into several levels, allowing you
to dig as deeply as you like for information and
insight.

The Knot
www.theknot.com
A wedding-planning website. Couples can create
a wedding website, register for gifts, and query
other couples on The Knot's message boards. This
site also has a sister website, www.thenest.com, for
newlyweds.

UltimateWedding.com
www.ultimatewedding.com
An all-encompassing wedding-planning website.
Includes tons of suggestions for everything from
the father-daughter dance to the wedding invitation
envelope seals.

Wedding Themes and More
www.wedthemes.com
A wedding-theme planning guide. Whether you're
thinking of having a celestial theme or a simply
romantic theme for your nuptials, this site will
help you incorporate that theme throughout your
special day.

Westchester Weddings—Planning and Idea Guide
www.westchester-weddings.com
Includes a section on wedding vows, with many suggested Bible verses, poetry, and sample vows. You'll also find lots of other valuable information for planning a wedding.

World Wedding Traditions
www.worldweddingtraditions.com
A resource for worldwide wedding customs and destination wedding planning.

Books

For more wedding vow samples, ceremony reading suggestions, and other wedding planning ideas, check out the following books.

Batts, Sidney F. *The Protestant Wedding Sourcebook*. Westminster/John Knox Press, 1993.

Lenderman, Teddy. *The Complete Idiot's Guide to the Perfect Wedding Illustrated, Fourth Edition*. Alpha Books, 2003.

Mayer, Gabrielle Kaplan. *The Creative Jewish Wedding Book*. Jewish Lights, 2004.

Metrick, Sydney Barbara. *I Do: A Guide to Creating You Own Unique Wedding Ceremony*. Celestial Arts Publishing, 1992.

Misner, Peter, and David Glusker, eds. *Words for Your Wedding: The Wedding Service Book*. Harper and Row, 1986.

Munro, Eleanor, ed. *Wedding Readings: Centuries of Writing and Rituals on Love and Marriage.* Penguin Books, 1996.

Roney, Carley. *The Knot Guide to Wedding Vows and Traditions.* Broadway Books, 2000.

Warner, Diane. *Complete Book of Wedding Vows.* Career Press, 1996.

Wright, H. Norman. *The Complete Book of Christian Wedding Vows: The Importance of How You Say "I Do."* Bethany House Publishers, 2003.

Index

D-E